Cambridge Elements ☰

Elements in The Aegean Bronze Age
edited by
Carl Knappett
University of Toronto
Irene Nikolakopoulou
Hellenic Ministry of Culture, Archaeological Museum of Heraklion

ECONOMY AND COMMODITY PRODUCTION IN THE AEGEAN BRONZE AGE

Catherine E. Pratt
The University of Texas at Austin

CAMBRIDGE
UNIVERSITY PRESS

Shaftesbury Road, Cambridge CB2 8EA, United Kingdom

One Liberty Plaza, 20th Floor, New York, NY 10006, USA

477 Williamstown Road, Port Melbourne, VIC 3207, Australia

314–321, 3rd Floor, Plot 3, Splendor Forum, Jasola District Centre, New Delhi – 110025, India

103 Penang Road, #05–06/07, Visioncrest Commercial, Singapore 238467

Cambridge University Press is part of Cambridge University Press & Assessment, a department of the University of Cambridge.

We share the University's mission to contribute to society through the pursuit of education, learning and research at the highest international levels of excellence.

www.cambridge.org
Information on this title: www.cambridge.org/9781009454674

DOI: 10.1017/9781009454681

First published 2025

A catalogue record for this publication is available from the British Library

ISBN 978-1-009-45467-4 Hardback
ISBN 978-1-009-45470-4 Paperback
ISSN 2754-2998 (online)
ISSN 2754-298X (print)

Cambridge University Press & Assessment has no responsibility for the persistence or accuracy of URLs for external or third-party internet websites referred to in this publication and does not guarantee that any content on such websites is, or will remain, accurate or appropriate.

Economy and Commodity Production in the Aegean Bronze Age

Elements in The Aegean Bronze Age

DOI: 10.1017/9781009454681
First published online: January 2025

Catherine E. Pratt
The University of Texas at Austin

Author for correspondence: Catherine E. Pratt,
catherine.pratt@austin.utexas.edu

Abstract: This Element does not discuss every aspect of the economy. Rather, it focuses on the first stage of an economic cycle – that of production. Two of the major guiding questions are: What products were the Bronze Age palatial states concerned with producing in surplus? And how did the palatial states control the production of these essential commodities? To answer these questions, the Element synthesizes previous work while interspersing its own conclusions on certain sub-topics, especially in light of recent archaeological data that help to fill out a picture incomplete based on textual evidence alone. With these goals in mind, this Element brings together both textual and archaeological data to reconstruct the internal economy and the production of commodities under the purview of Minoan and Mycenaean palatial states.

Keywords: Minoan, economy, Mycenaean, production, Mediterranean

ISBNs: 9781009454674 (HB), 9781009454704 (PB), 9781009454681 (OC)
ISSNs: 2754-2998 (online), 2754-298X (print)

Contents

1 Introduction

The Aegean Bronze Age economy is a vast topic with a long history of scholarship. It should not come as a surprise, then, for me to preface this Element by saying that I do not intend to discuss every aspect of the economy (in whatever way we want to define it), nor do I intend to present an entirely novel analysis of the complex networks of transactions among people and things that made up the "economy." Instead, I will narrow down my focus to the internal economy of the Minoan and Mycenaean palatial eras. Specifically, this Element is concerned with the first stage of an economic cycle – that of production. Two of the major guiding questions are: What types of products were the Bronze Age palatial states concerned with producing in surplus? And by what mechanisms did the palatial states control the production of these essential commodities? By focusing on the local economies of Aegean states, this element is complementary to others in this series, including Sarah Murray's (2023) discussion of long-distance exchange and interregional economies. The following text endeavors to synthesize much of what has been written on the topic, including both foundational work and newer additions to the bibliography. And, in doing so, I hope to produce a useful document for scholars, from specialists in Linear B to students interested in the mythological time of Heroes. I will, of course, intersperse throughout this Element my own conclusions on certain subtopics, especially in light of recent archaeological data that help to fill out a picture considerably incomplete based on textual evidence alone. With these goals in mind, the following narrative brings together both textual and archaeological data to reconstruct the internal economy and the production of commodities under the purview of Minoan and Mycenaean palatial states.

2 Commodity Production

Production of commodities is a key component of most economies. No matter the scale, from household to empire, production is necessary for the functioning of economic transactions. You must have something with which you can trade, barter, gift, and so on. And, at a basic human level, you must produce something to eat (or something you can exchange for food). This section explores the local production of Bronze Age Aegean societies. Some relevant questions include: What types of commodities were produced on a large scale? Which commodities were a focal point of palatial enterprise? Which were not? Non-agricultural products are mentioned, and sometimes regulated to a high degree; they played a major role in the functioning of palatial economies. However, agricultural goods make up most of the products visible archaeologically and recorded in texts, so this is where my focus falls – especially those mentioned frequently in Bronze Age texts. Here, *agricultural goods* are defined as *domesticated plants, animals, and materials derived directly from them*. I will nonetheless comment on non-agrarian goods when enough data are present.

One key methodological consideration is the relative weight given to textual sources and bioarchaeological remains (e.g. Livarda & Kotzamani 2013; Halstead 2003). The second concerns the differing values attributed to agrarian products, with some produced for subsistence, while others hold cultural significance. I use the idea of entanglement to better understand *why* a particular thing might or might not have been valued (Pratt 2021). Entanglement describes the complex relationships generated between people and things over time.[1] Specifically, the relationships between people and things can be designated as ones of dependence (pl. dependences) or dependency (pl. dependencies). Dependence suggests a positive relationship whereby the one gains something through the presence of the other, whereas dependency suggests a more negative relationship whereby the one could not survive without the other. For example, bread/free-threshing wheat might be a product engendering dependence, not dependency. It was perhaps socially significant to have leavened loaves, but not necessary for the proper functioning of hierarchies, rituals, and economic exchanges. As we will see, archaeobotanical remains suggest grain might have been purposefully mixed. Other than bread/free-threshing wheat, the difference between barley, emmer wheat, and einkorn might not have been very significant. In any event, the value of wheat arose from the complex entanglements between people and things.

Commodities that stand out from the rest due to their deep entanglement and subsequent high value take on a new role that I define as "cultural commodities."[2] Cultural commodities lie at the intersection of value, exchange, and dependency, where discontinuation is no longer an option because of the long history of increasing entanglement. Cultural commodities can be considered in opposition to subsistence commodities. In other words, they are both needed and wanted. Ultimately, cultural commodities become signifiers of identity, deeply rooted in social and ideological practices. I have argued elsewhere (Pratt 2021) that olive oil and wine became cultural commodities during the Bronze Age.

---

[1] On "entanglement" more generally, see Hodder 2012.

[2] See Pratt 2021: 10–17 for a thorough discussion of this concept. From a Marxist perspective, a commodity is something that has both use value and exchange value (Jung 2021). Here, since I am not specifically taking a Marxist perspective, I will use the term "commodity" relatively interchangeably with "product," unless otherwise specified.

These considerations feature in the following sections through a diachronic analysis spanning the Minoan Neopalatial,[3] Mycenaean palatial,[4] and Postpalatial eras.[5] By focusing on patterns in relative quantities of different types of products and the way those products were regulated, we can get a better idea of the shifting values attributed to specific commodities, ways of organizing labor, and consumption practices.

2.1 Data and Their Limitations

In what follows, I draw from both archaeological and written evidence, when available. Minoan (undeciphered) texts written in Linear A provide a more limited, yet parallel, source of data to the Mycenaean Linear B texts, which are more plentiful, though not without their challenges. Linear A texts are extremely limited in number and vary greatly from site to site. Their preservation was purely by chance and they therefore represent a small fraction of what was clearly a complex record-keeping system. Moreover, the types of texts preserved and their subjects are also haphazard. Since Linear A is undeciphered, we can only make educated guesses concerning the structure of their records, including texts dealing with outgoing versus incoming versus in-store products. In addition, different locations might have had different administrative practices, which could potentially skew our interpretations of specific words and patterns between sites. Nevertheless, we can still gain some meaningful insights about the products listed on these tablets and their relative quantities. Even Linear B tablets, deciphered and much more plentiful, suffer from the same dilemmas. The administrative contexts of extant texts differ from site to site, which makes comparison more challenging. In addition, groups of texts date to different destruction events, and therefore represent different time periods.[6]

However, the main issues here concern the types of products and their scale of production. When all extant tablets are considered together some of the problems already highlighted are mitigated. Even though most grain records at Pylos come from ration tablets, we can get a sense of the scale of production of grain compared to figs, oil, and wine. While it is true that not all tablets are equal and some might record outgoing versus incoming products, or even products that are

---

[3] Although there is a Protopalatial period or "Old Palace" period on Crete, here I will focus mainly on the Linear A documents of Neopalatial Crete. MM IIIA-LM IB in ceramic chronology; roughly 1750–1460 BCE.

[4] Predominantly the Late Helladic period on the mainland and Monopalatial/Final Palatial period on Crete; LH II-IIIB (mainland) and LM II-LM III (Crete) in ceramic chronology; roughly 1400–1200 BCE.

[5] Predominantly the LH/LM IIIC period; roughly 1200–1050 BCE.

[6] For example, there were multiple conflagrations that preserved the Linear B texts from LM II-III Knossos. For more on the timing and locations of Linear B tablets, see notes 47 and 48.

missing, the quantities present indicate administrative control. In other words, adding up the product quantities denoted at a given site might not constitute the total stores available at a particular time within palatial walls. It does, however, represent the total amount of a particular good over which the palace has control in one way or another. Certainly, there will be overlaps and some inaccuracies. However, I would argue that since all of the products discussed here are treated equivalently, total quantities present on extant tablets can still provide some meaningful insights into the relative volumes, values, and regulation of specific commodities.

Despite the inherent limitations of contemporary Bronze Age texts, I steer away from using later Classical texts and modern analogies to preserve an emic (Bronze Age) perspective, as far as is possible. The environment, both generally and in its microclimatic variations, fluctuated greatly over centuries and was arguably very different during the Late Bronze Age than today. To use modern Mediterranean cultures as a means of understanding Bronze Age hierarchies of value and production strategies undermines the significance of individual cultural variation through time and space. Food is a significant aspect of cultural identity; we cannot assume the food practices of one culture apply to another. In keeping with this idea, I minimize the use of contemporaneous analogies from neighboring cultures. Hittite, Egyptian, and even Levantine production strategies, distribution mechanisms, and consumption practices were necessarily different from those on Minoan Crete or the Mycenaean mainland.

Similarly, I attempt to keep palatial and non-palatial data separate. Although this is difficult to accomplish in the Minoan period, given that the definition of "palace" is hazy at best, it is easier in the Mycenaean period.[7] Ideally, we should avoid using palaeobotanical evidence from contemporary Late Bronze Age non-palatial or rural sites to try and understand palatial values or use of commodities. There will be a necessary connection between the hinterland and the palace, but not all commodities that are found in rural sites receive the same attention in a palatial context. Excavations have focused predominantly on palatial sites and those sites have produced the vast majority of (Linear B) texts. While it is recognized that the palaces were only one node in a much larger economic network, they nevertheless became the focal point of much research on Bronze Age economic practices. Individuals are the foundation of an economy, so wherever possible I have included prosopographical information related to Mycenaean production, distribution, and

---

[7] As discussed in Section 3, court-centered buildings once thought of as "palaces" in Minoan Crete are now generally regarded as something very different from the traditional concept. Moreover, most Linear A tablets do not come from court-centered buildings but from elsewhere, including "villas" and other noncanonical buildings.

consumption.[8] Archaeological, and especially palaeobotanical, evidence is more widespread, but limited in scope and varied in methodology. The preservation of perishable materials is sparse in Greece and, when available, has received very different treatment depending on when the material was excavated and the goals of sampling strategies. Recently, much more emphasis has been placed on palaeobotanical research and quality publications for the last thirty years or so are available (and referenced frequently here).[9] Thus, a holistic and up-to-date approach to data available for understanding Bronze Age Aegean domestic production is presented.

By comparing different periods, I aim to evaluate regimes of value side by side within the context of a cultural economy paradigm. Production in vast quantities could signal use for rations, or equally payments, or offerings. Commodities produced in small quantities might be reserved for elite or divine purposes. Through this comparative approach, we can see how the value of these commodities changes, in part through their quantities, as well as their changing use from one regime to the next.

3 Minoan Palatial Era

The Minoan Palatial Era encompasses the Protopalatial, or First Palace, and Neopalatial, or Second Palace, periods and spans roughly 450 years (ca. 1900–1450 BCE).[10] Because the second palaces were often built on top of the ruins of the first, we naturally know less about the earlier periods of these structures. To even call them "palaces" is problematic and mostly a hold-over from their initial discovery at the beginning of the twentieth century. Since then, most scholars have moved away from the idea that these impressive buildings were seats of kings and queens and more towards an interpretation as communal and/or religious spaces run by a group of people.[11] To avoid instinctual assumptions implied by the word "palace," the descriptive term "court-centered building" is often used. Here, I will use the term "palace" in a general sense, especially when referring to administration, and "court-centered building" for specific sites. Clues to the administration of these central places are provided by clay tablets

---

[8] See work by Nakassis 2006, 2013, 2015.

[9] See, for Minoan Crete, e.g., Livarda & Kotzamani 2013, 2020, Tsafou & García-Granero 2021, Sarpaki 2007; for Mycenaean Greece see, e.g., Valamoti et al. 2022, Margaritis et al. 2014, Pasternak 2006; for Postpalatial era see, e.g., Schachl 2006, Halstead et al. 2022, Livarda & Kotzamani 2006, Kroll 2000. Henkel & Margaritis 2024 was unable to be included in this publication due to the timing of release; however, it is added here as a very comprehensive reference for the archaeobotany of Prehistoric Crete.

[10] For more information on absolute vs. relative dating and the ongoing debate between high and low chronology see citations in Salgarella 2020: 1, n. 2.

[11] Driessen 2018.

and nodules on which were recorded various economic affairs. The language of the people living on Crete, however, is not known and the scripts in which it was written, predominantly Cretan Hieroglyphic during the Protopalatial period and Linear A during the Neopalatial, are undeciphered.[12] Here, I will focus mainly on the Neopalatial period and documents written in Linear A for a few reasons. The first is that there are fewer documents preserved written in Cretan Hieroglyphic and therefore less is known about the administration of the first palaces.[13] The second is that, based on what is already known, there seem to be significant differences in the ways in which the Old Palaces and New Palaces were governed, and it would therefore be misleading to blend information from both phases. Finally, by using the later Linear B script as a guide, scholars have been able to identify certain ideograms (pictures standing for words/ideas),[14] and phonetic values of many Linear A signs, as well as numerals, and measures (both liquid and dry) used in the Linear A script.[15] The information available from these tablets is therefore more robust.[16] Most of the identifiable ideograms are agricultural in nature and therefore help us to understand quantities of certain commodities and which resources were handled in specialized ways. Numerals on Linear A tablets are particularly helpful, but need to be converted to absolute quantities in order to make sense of the data. There has been significant debate over the Minoan system of whole and fractional units and their relationship to absolute volumes in both dry and liquid measures.[17] Here, I rely on the absolute quantities assigned to units in Schoep (2002: 94) and Palmer (1995: 137), ultimately derived from Lang (1964) through Ventris & Chadwick (1973), with one whole dry measurement equating to 96 liters and one whole liquid measurement equating to 28.8 liters.[18]

---

[12] The two coexist for a time in the Protopalatial period.

[13] For more on Cretan Hieroglyphic script, see Olivier & Godart 1996; Jasink 2009; Decorte 2017. There is great debate over the chronological and geographical use of this script (Decorte 2018; Ferrara, Montecchi, & Valério 2022). Fewer than 400 inscriptions in Cretan Hieroglyphic have been found, compared to around 1,500 Linear A inscriptions (Steele 2024: xiv from Perna 2014: 253).

[14] The term "ideogram" is generally interchangeable with "logogram" and its preference depends on the author. See, e.g., Thompson 2010.

[15] For Linear A administration in general, see Schoep 2002; for the development of Linear B from Linear A see Steele 2024: 1–14.

[16] Here, I also focus mostly on the Linear A *tablets* for data on production. The inscriptions on sealed documents using roundels seems to be of a different nature from the inscriptions on tablets. For example, most single-hole hanging nodules have only a single sign on one side (836 out of a total of 878 preserved nodules; Schoep 2002: 40, table 1.7). For information on Linear A nodules, roundels, and sealings see Schoep 2002: 40–43; Hallager 2000.

[17] For more on absolute values of units see: De Fidio 2024a (weight) and De Fidio 2024b (volume).

[18] These are the same absolute quantities often assigned to the units in Linear B, and are here (as in Schoep 2002 and Palmer 1995) used for comparative purposes. It is generally assumed that units listed on different tablets and from different sites are comparable (Palmer 1995: 137). These absolute quantities are by no means agreed-upon, and differing opinions abound.

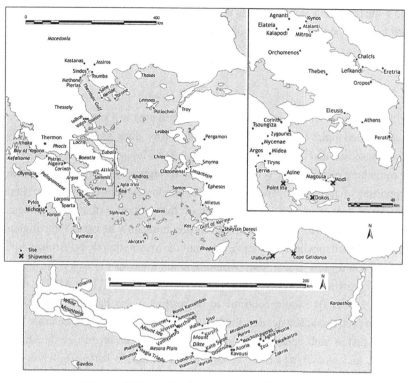

Figure 1 Map with sites mentioned in the text.

Unlike later Linear B tablets, Linear A tablets have been found both inside and outside court-centered buildings. Indeed, there seems to be little difference between the administration of a so-called "villa" like Hagia Triada and a court-centered building like Zakros (Schoep 2002: 89; Montecchi 2019). Thirteen sites on Crete and three in the Cyclades have produced Linear A tablets, but only three sites on Crete have produced enough to reveal any meaningful patterns in production: Hagia Triada (147 tablets and fragments), Chania (93 tablets and fragments), and Zakros (31 tablets and fragments; Figure 1).[19] Within these tablets, five agricultural commodities stand out for their high frequency and large quantity: grain (AB 120), figs (AB 30), olives (AB 122), olive oil (A 302),

---

See, e.g. Montecchi (2019: 109) and De Fidio (2024b: 203–4) for alternative suggestions. It is interesting to note that even in this latest publication, De Fidio (2024b: 203) suggests a new reading of 48 liters for dry and 14.4 for liquid units (i.e. half of what is adopted in Palmer 1995 and Schoep 2002), but Volume two of the same work (Killen 2024) uses the old values from Ventris and Chadwick 1973 (120 liters for dry; 36 liters for liquid units) in its translations.

[19] Palmer 1995: 134; Schoep 2002. Even between these sites, preservation of the tablets is not equal and likely affects the amount of data we can meaningfully extrapolate. Tablets from Chania and Phaistos are more poorly preserved than those from Haghia Triada and Zakros (Schoep 2002: 39).

and wine (AB 131). Although less prominent, animals and their byproducts, as well as some non-agricultural goods played a role in Neopalatial production.

3.1 Agricultural Goods

3.1.1 Grain

Within the study of agricultural products represented in Linear A, one of the most debated topics is which grain is represented by ideogram AB 120. There is wide consensus that it is a grain of some kind, but whether it is barley or wheat, or something else entirely, is uncertain. Various arguments have been put forth supporting mainly barley or wheat. A common assumption since the first discovery and attempted decipherment of these texts is that it represents wheat (Palmer 1992: 475–76). This bias is predominantly because of the higher value attributed to wheat by later Greeks and the assumption that if Bronze Age Cretans could grow wheat, they would. Certain areas of the island are better suited to growing wheat, which takes more care and water.[20] That AB 120 (and *120 in Linear B) should continue to be read as wheat has been argued by Halstead (2001) and Halstead et al. (2022), although he is quick to concede that it could just as well be any other grain, considering that bread/free-threshing, einkorn, and emmer wheat have been found alongside barley, bitter vetch, lentils, and other types of peas and legumes in archaeobotanical remains (see Section 3.1.7). On the other hand, Palmer (1992, 1995, 2002, 2008) has argued convincingly that AB 120, and therefore 120* in Linear B, should be read as barley. Based on the large quantities noted, its use for rations, and ubiquity of AB 120, Palmer suggests that barley works better as AB 120. This suggestion has been followed by others (e.g. Schoep 2002; Montecchi 2019), but is not secure. Indeed, barley and emmer wheat are just about evenly accounted for in the archaeological record and are often found together in specific contexts, as discussed at the end of this section. Could it be that AB 120 stands for a more generic "grain" and its many ligatures designate specifically what type of grain is being recorded? And, if there is no ligature, perhaps it does not matter in that particular record what type of grain is being collected or distributed? There are no clear indications that specific grains were always treated differently in the Bronze Age as they were in later historical periods. Emmer wheat and barley might have been considered relatively similar in status and functional

---

[20] Nitsch et al. 2019 analyzed LM II grains from Knossos with the result that the emmer wheat sampled appears better watered than the sampled barley grains. The implication is that the palace administration was concerned with the irrigation of wheat. They concluded that wheat was therefore the most likely grain represented by *120 in the Linear B archives, and hence AB 120 in the Linear A (2019: 160). However, care does not necessarily mean increased scale.

capabilities, as opposed to, say, free-threshing wheat with its ability to produce leavened bread. Lacking a clear solution to this problem, I will use the word "grain" when discussing AB 120.

Grain is by far the most copious commodity present in Linear A texts. At Hagia Triada alone, grain is mentioned eighty-two times and at least 474,369.6 total liters are indicated.[21] In keeping with the smaller number of documents preserved, only 10,373+ liters of AB 120 are recorded at Chania, and 14,976+ liters at Zakros. In addition, 1,920+ liters have been noted at the villa of Archanes, and 480+ liters at Knossos (KN 28a), as well as one AB 120 ideogram on a roundel at Malia (see Table 1). While we do not know for certain the period of time represented by these records, one season is generally assumed. The disparity in quantities at Hagia Triada, Zakros, and Chania can also be partly ascribed to the number and preservation of the tablets themselves, as well as their find-spots. Tablets from Chania are quite fragmentary, whereas those from Hagia Triada and Zakros are relatively more intact (Schoep 2002: 39). We could therefore assume that much more grain would have been recorded at Zakros and Chania on tablets that no longer exist or have not yet been excavated. To put it into context, the large quantity of grain at Hagia Triada, 474,369.6+ liters, is almost seven times more than the second most represented commodity, figs (69,408+ liters).[22] So, based on the surviving tablets, grain is the most dominant agricultural product recorded in Linear A texts. Moreover, at Hagia Triada nine tablets are solely dedicated to recording grain entries and range from 480+ to 101,760 liters. It should be emphasized, however, that not every entry of grain on the tablets is huge. Indeed, when grain appears alongside other commodities (on twenty-eight tablets), amounts range from less than 96 liters to 120,384 liters (Palmer 1995). In these mixed commodity tablets, grain almost always has the largest quantity and is listed first in each section. The tablets that might indicate totals of grain received could represent crops collected from various localities as taxes or contributions of some kind (Palmer 1995: 147; Schoep 2002: 180).

We should also note that AB 120 has many variants in Linear A (the ideogram plus ligatures). At Hagia Triada, fourteen variants are recorded. At Chania, two

---

[21] As noted earlier, all absolute numbers derive from equating one dry unit with 96 liters and one liquid unit with 28.8 liters. Table 1 outlines all quantities mentioned in the text and units of a particular ideogram are derived from Schoep 2002 and Montecchi 2019, unless otherwise stated. Here, I will also reiterate what was stated earlier, namely that these numbers are for comparative purposes only and are necessarily inaccurate due to the undeciphered and complex nature of Linear A tablets, which include quantities of items incoming, outgoing, and assessed and therefore have the potential to overlap.

[22] For more discussion on the tablets that include AB 120 at Hagia Triada, see Montecchi 2019: 115–26.

Table 1 Number of attestations of specific Linear A ideograms on Neopalatial tablets and the minimum total amount of the commodity in liters.

	AB 120 + ligatures (Barley?)	A 303** (Wheat?)	AB 30 (Figs)	AB 122 (Olives)	A 302 + ligatures (Oil)	AB 131a–c (Wine)
Hagia Triada	82* (474,369.6+ liters)	20 (7,968+ liters)	32 (69,408+ liters)	14 (16,608+ liters)	96 (13,881.6+ liters)	28 (17,568+ liters)
Chania	7 (10,272+ liters)	67 (4,608 liters)	14 (3,552+ liters)	0	9 (878.4 + liters)	11 (86.4+ liters)
Zakros	14 (14,976+ liters)	0	2 (5,416+ liters)	5 (2,712+ liters)	1 (Quantity: fractional)	9 (7,516.8+ liters)
Archanes	4 (1,920+ liters)	0	0	1 (288+ liters)	2 (115.2 liters)	4 (28.8+ liters)
Tylissos	0	0	0	1 (384 liters)	16 (ca. 3,965.5 liters)	0

Knossos	1 (480+ liters)	0	0	0	1 (no associated numerals)
Kato Symi	0	0	1 (no associated numerals)	0	0
Myrtos-Pyrgos	0	0	0	0	1 (ca. 2,592 liters)
Malia	1 (roundel)	0	0	0	0

Calculations are based on tablets listed in Schoep 2002, 97, 100, 103, 110, and 119. Schoep 2002, 102, 182, and 184 shows conflicting amounts for ZA 4. Page 184 lists the amount of wine on ZA 4 as 9,984 liters, about sixty-five pithoi. This seems to be a mistake, using dry instead of liquid measurements. Calculations for commodities from Hagia Triada are from Montecchi 2019, 126, 134, 138–9, 145, 151, 155. All totals are estimations and often do not include fractional signs, the values for which are unknown. Common fractional signs were calculated from Schoep 2002, 32, table 1.4, after Bennett 1950, fig. 2.

* The total can be broken down into: AB 120: 3,655 units = 350,880 liters; [AB 120]: 148 units = 14,208 liters; and AB 120 plus ligatures: 1,532 units = 147,072 liters

** A 303 mostly occurs in fractions of units. While the absolute quantities are unknown, their relative values are much smaller than a single total unit, and therefore represent much smaller absolute quantities.

variants are recorded, both of which also appear at Hagia Triada. Zakros also has two variants, but they are different. The meaning behind these variants is unclear, but are likely to comment on a type of grain, an intrinsic quality such as whether the grain has been processed, the quality of the land on which it was grown, or its intention as food or fodder (Schoep 2002: 180).

At least one other ideogram should be mentioned in the context of grain production. The identification of A 303 as an agricultural product is generally accepted. Based on the smaller quantities listed and the use of the ideogram within Linear A texts, Palmer (1992, 1995) suggests that it might represent emmer wheat. Schoep (2002) agrees this is likely but suggests it could also represent archaeologically attested legumes. A 303 occurs sixty-seven times at Chania, but the total only amounts to ca. 4,608 liters. At Hagia Triada, it is listed twenty times and amounts to 7,968+ liters.[23] So, even though it is most frequently mentioned at Chania, the total quantity suggests it was a high-value or difficult commodity to produce. Free-threshing wheat or, perhaps more likely, wheat flour would account for the smaller quantities. That it was a processed agricultural commodity might also be supported by the large number of variants (eight) associated with the ideogram.

In keeping with its prominence in Linear A tablets, grain is also the most frequently attested plant type found in archaeobotanical records (Livarda & Kotzamani 2013; Halstead et al. 2022). What is interesting is that wheat and barley are just about tied for their frequency of appearance. Many different forms of wheat and barley are attested since the Neolithic period on Crete: glume wheats (einkorn, emmer), free-threshing wheat, and hulled and naked barley. Out of twelve archaeobotanical records dating to the Neopalatial period, six had wheat, five had barley, and one was unidentified (Livarda & Kotzamani 2013: 10, fig. 6). Of the wheats, emmer was the most common, showing up in five out of twelve samples. This is followed by hulled barley in three out of twelve samples. The remaining samples included two with free-threshing wheat, one with einkorn, and one with millet. In their overview of all the available archaeobotanical material from Bronze Age Cretan sites, Livarda and Kotzamani suggest that "hulled barley, emmer, and free-threshing wheat are the only cereals that have been found as deliberately cultivated crops" (2013: 10). All of the other types might be intrusions. Indeed, based on the discovery of free-threshing wheat in Neolithic levels of Knossos, Livarda and Kotzamani (2013: 11) suggest this particular product might have been a specialty of the region and indicates an early contact with the east, where sites like Neolithic Çatalhöyük had been already cultivating this crop for a few hundred

---

[23] For more discussion on the tablets that include A 303 at Hagia Triada, see Montecchi 2019: 151–55.

years. This archaeobotanical emphasis on wheat might lend more weight to the identification of AB 120 with this commodity and its variety of forms.

3.1.2 Figs

Perhaps surprisingly, figs, represented by ideogram AB 30, are the second most prevalent foodstuff after grain (AB 120) in the Linear A tablets. At Hagia Triada, figs are mentioned on at least thirty-two tablets and amount to 69,408+ liters.[24] At Chania, figs are recorded fourteen times and amount to 3,552+ liters and at Zakros, they are mentioned only two times, but record 5,416+ liters (see Table 1). Indeed, figs are more prominent in the Linear A texts than olives. Tablets from Hagia Triada's Casa del Lebete list figs as part of distribution lists. Here, and in other contexts, figs are listed alongside A 303 (possibly wheat or wheat flour, see Section 3.1.1) and wine (Schoep 2002: 184–85). Other mixed commodity tablets feature figs along with barley. On these tablets, the quantity of figs is usually one-half to one-third the amount of barley (Palmer 1995: 148). They could be interpreted as either contribution or distribution lists.

On four tablets from Hagia Triada, figs are treated separately and appear in the heading of a section of what might be "totaling tablets." Two totaling tablets list figs in large quantities: HT 131 (92 units; 8,832 liters) and HT 67 (400 units; 38,400 liters). Thus, figs seem to be an important commodity to palatial interests and the production of large quantities was expected. Palatial interest in the production of figs is also supported by a tablet from Zakros. On ZA 8, figs are the only commodity listed with seven entries that range from 94 to 384+ liters. Interestingly, AB 30 has no variants or ligatures, unlike all of the other commodities discussed here. What could the lack of variants suggest? They are listed in the same contexts as other foodstuffs, so variants are unlikely to indicate a part of the bureaucratic system. Instead, it might suggest that figs were not considered as having differing qualities, flavors, or varieties. Figs, likely dried, were accepted as a whole fruit. Archaeologically, whole figs have been found in the Hagia Triada's "Casa dei Ficchi" together with remains of wheat, barley, chickpeas, Cyperus, and lentils (Follieri 1979–1980: 165–72).[25]

3.1.3 Olives

Olives, represented by ideogram AB 122 are frequently listed in Linear A tablets and are the third-largest total quantity of foodstuffs at Hagia Triada.

---

[24] For more on fig entries on the Hagia Triada tablets, see Montecchi 2019: 139–46.

[25] See Pratt (in preparation) for a detailed analysis of fig cultivation and use in the Aegean Bronze Age.

There, olives are listed fourteen times and amount to 16,608+ liters.[26] Interestingly, they are not found on the records from Chania but are listed five times at Zakros with a total of 2,712+ liters. They are also listed once at the villa of Archanes (288+ liters), once at Tylissos (384 liters) and once at Kato Symi with no associated numerals (see Table 1). The lack of olives at Chania is likely due to the small number of texts and their specific purposes, not to the lack of olives in the landscape. At Hagia Triada, AB 122 and one variant appear on eleven mixed commodity tablets, most frequently alongside barley, olive oil, and A 304, an unidentified agricultural commodity. The amounts of olives listed range from less than 96 liters to 8,928+ liters. In half of these tablets, the quantities of olives listed are around the same as the quantities of the other goods listed, except for grain (AB 120), which is always larger (Palmer 1995). At Zakros, olives are listed on three tablets in quantities of 2,400+ liters, 288 liters, and less than 96 liters. Olives listed in Linear A texts might be for eating rather than oil production, since olive oil has its own ideogram and was likely processed outside of administrative centers (Schoep 2002: 184). It is also interesting that only one variant has been identified for olives, placing it closer to figs as a whole fruit. Grain, olive oil, and wine receive over fourteen, fourteen, and five variants, respectively, as processed agricultural products.

3.1.4 Olive Oil

The ideogram for olive oil in Linear A was not as easily identified but is now generally accepted to be A 302.[27] Interestingly, olive oil has the highest number of entries at Hagia Triada (96) but amounts to ca. 13,881.6 liters.[28] When compared to grain, which is listed eighty-two times with a total of 474,369.6 liters, it is clear that olive oil was generally collected or used in frequent, small quantities, whereas grain was collected or used in frequent, and sometimes very large quantities. At Chania, olive oil is listed nine times with a total of at least 878 liters, again suggesting frequent, small entries. Olive oil is only listed once at Zakros in a small fractional quantity, less than 96 liters (see Table 1). Like the lack of olive entries at Chania, this is likely attributed to the small number of tablets recovered from Zakros, rather than a general trend. At Hagia Triada, two (or possibly three) tablets are single-commodity tablets dealing solely with olive oil and list large quantities (HT 2: ca. 490 liters; HT 42 ca. 576 liters; and HT 8 ca. 4,060 liters). On twenty-nine mixed commodity tablets, olive oil quantities range from less than 28.8 liters to 576 liters.

---

[26] For more on olives in the tablets at Hagia Triada, see Montecchi 2019: 146–51.

[27] For the identification, see Palaima 1994: 304–5; Palmer 1995: 135.

[28] For further discussion of olive oil on the tablets from at Hagia Triada, see Montecchi 2019: 126–34.

Similar to olives, olive oil is also listed on tablets found in other contexts. It is listed twice at the villa of Archanes (115.2 liters) and sixteen times at Tylissos (ca. 3,965.5 liters; see Table 1). It is perhaps significant that these two large villas list both olives and olive oil, and at Tylissos, at least, a relatively large total quantity of olive oil. It might support the idea that central administrations were much less concerned with olives than with receiving the value-added product of the fruit – namely, various types of olive oil – which was processed in the countryside closer to the orchards themselves. As discussed in Section 3.3, Minoan central administrations seem to be generally unconcerned with control of production of agricultural products as long as they receive necessary quantities of the final commodity, whatever that might be (processed grain, olive oil, wine, and dried figs). Olive oil is mostly listed in large, whole numbers, which might support these entries as incoming rather than outgoing quantities (Schoep 2002: 182).

Another distinctive feature of olive oil in Linear A texts is that it is associated with many different ligatures. At Hagia Triada, fourteen variants are found and at Chania, two variants are listed, both of which are also found at Hagia Triada. This overlap would suggest that not all ligatures were specific to a particular administration system, but rather were general designations endemic to the Linear A writing system. In addition, A 302 usually appears with more than one ligature per tablet and in more than one section per tablet. A large number of variants of A 302 occur repeatedly, much more than the variants of AB 120 or AB 131, which might imply that the information encoded in the ligature was considered natural or essential to the collection of the different forms of olive oil (Palmer 1995: 141). Ligatured forms might refer to an intrinsic quality, type of oil, or different scents. The appearance of multiple variants alongside one another might support the idea that they represent different scents. Scented oil was an important commodity in the Mediterranean more generally, and in Aegean Bronze Age societies specifically. On Minoan Crete, potential per-fumed oil workshops have been identified at higher-order sites like Mochlos (Brogan & Koh 2008).

3.1.5 Wine

Wine was an important commodity in Linear A texts, as attested by the frequency of its ideogram (AB 131a–c) at many different sites. Following figs, it is the fourth most frequently listed commodity at Hagia Triada (28 entries) and totals at least 17,568 liters, similar in quantity to olive oil.[29] Unlike olive oil, however, wine entries are in much greater amounts. At Hagia Triada, wine is listed on three

---

[29] For more on the tablets at Hagia Triada that mention wine, see Montecchi 2019: 134–39.

single commodity tablets along with a word (AB04/TE) that seems to indicate the large-scale collection of wine (Schoep 2002: 184). The amounts on these tablets range from 1,526.4 liters to over 3,744 liters. On sixteen other tablets, wine appears alongside other commodities with amounts ranging from less than 28.8 liters to 4,233.6 liters. A unique tablet, HT 27, begins like a normal personnel or commodity tablet but in the last two sections, it only lists varieties of wine with quantities per entry ranging from 28.8 to 2,016 liters.

At Chania, wine is listed eleven times but only totals 86 liters. In contrast, tablets from Zakros list wine only nine times, but total 7,516 liters (see Table 1). Again, it is unclear whether this discrepancy is due to differences in preservation or whether Zakros specialized in wine production. At Zakros, four tablets are dedicated to wine as a single commodity with ZA 4 listing 2,995.2 liters and ZA 15 listing 2,736 liters. Significantly, the majority of tablets dealing with wine at Zakros were not found at the palace, but in "mansions" located in the associated town. AB 131a is also found on the rim of a pithos jar (ZA Zb 3) alongside a number indicating 921.6 liters and within an inscription indicating a giver and recipient (Davis 2013: 47).

The wine ideogram is also listed four times at Archanes (ca. 28.8 liters), twice at Phaistos (57.6 liters), once at Myrtos-Pyrgos (ca. 2,592 liters), and once at Knossos (no associated numerals; Table 1). The ubiquity of the wine ideogram might suggest that wine was not socially or palatially restricted. The ideogram for wine comes in three versions (131a, 131b, and 131c) and also has associated ligatures. Unlike the variants of other commodities, the three versions of ideogram AB 131 are formed by altering the shape of the sign itself. At Hagia Triada, five variants are found. Some scholars have suggested AB 131b should be translated as vinegar, but the identity of 131c is unknown (Palmer 1994: 88–91). At Zakros, ZA 10 has a section headed by AB 131c with 10 entries below adding up to 1,123.2 liters. This would be a significant amount of vinegar. Its designation as vinegar is derived predominantly from later Linear B ideograms for wine and this particular version's association with perfume manufacture. Alternatively, the versions of the sign and their ligatures could designate age or even flavor.

3.1.6 Animals

Perhaps surprisingly, animals are not often accounted for in Linear A texts. Compared to such large quantities of plant-based commodities, animals, and their related goods (meat, wool, and cheese) are hardly ever recorded.[30] When

---

[30] Of course, we can't discount the possibility that tablets recording livestock accounts were not preserved at these sites. Earlier (MM II) Cretan Hieroglyphic tablets from Protopalatial Malia

they are recorded, animals are listed in small numbers and likely represent offerings to particular people or gods for specific occasions. Livestock identified in Linear A tablets includes sheep (AB 21), goats (AB 22), cattle (AB 23), and pigs (AB 85).[31] At Hagia Triada, among all the tablets, there are only three sheep, thirty-one pigs, eight bulls, and possibly six goats listed.[32] To illustrate their contexts in mixed commodity tablets, HT 38 lists three sheep and one pig along with one vase and two kinds of cloth. At Chania, five tablets record animals listed in ones and twos. Again, these are more likely one-time occasions or deliveries, rather than a large-scale production controlled by the palatial authorities. Only at Zakros is there some indication that groups of animals were of palatial concern, specifically sheep. Here, sheep appear in three varieties on three single commodity tablets (ZA 9, 22, and 26) with lists of herds from different places. The final entry on ZA 22 lists 100 female sheep. However, in the context of the broader Aegean Bronze Age, these are still very small numbers. In the following discussion of Mycenaean production, sheep, for example, are listed in the tens-of-thousands (see Section 4.1.6).

One possible explanation for the lack of palatial interest in animal flocks is that they were more concerned with secondary products related to those animals. Specifically, there are some entries that might record wool (A 556–563) and textiles (AB 54, AB 164). At Hagia Triada, one tablet (HT 24) lists large quantities of wool, perhaps 46 kg.[33] This particular tablet was found near Room 27 of the villa where numerous loom weights were also discovered along with 45 noduli on the window sill, which might have been connected with this particular transaction (Palaima 1994: 317; Schoep 2002: 187). Although recorded in small quantities, textiles are listed in three different varieties: plain, with the addition of "KU," and with the addition of "ZO." Interestingly, these varieties will be carried forward into the Linear B archives of the later Mycenaean period. A tablet fragment from Complex Delta at Akrotiri on the nearby island of Thera (modern Santorini) lists 200 units of textiles and was found alongside many loomweights (Boulotis 1998: 407–11). These examples support the idea that the Neopalatial palaces and central buildings had less concern with the maintenance of flocks and more concern

---

might record much larger numbers of animals (Oliver & Godart 1996: 142, 146, 152, 156, 170; Alberti et al. 2019: 53).

[31] Archaeological faunal remains corroborate the species listed in the tablets. For example, sheep, goats, pigs, and cattle are reported at Mochlos, but pigs and cows are absent at Pseira (Christakis 2019: 44).

[32] However, HT 30.4.5 might list 100 oxen, which would be a large number of beasts even for Mycenaean standards (Palaima 1992: 463–74; Schoep 2002: 187). On animals in the texts at Hagia Triada in general, see Montecchi 2019: 182–88.

[33] On wool and textiles in the Hagia Triada texts in general, see Montecchi 2019: 196–203.

with the accumulation of secondary productions, such as wool, and its transformation into valuable textiles.

3.1.7 Other Foodstuffs

The list of other archaeologically attested food from the Neopalatial archaeological record is long and includes pulses (lentils, peas, and beans), other animal meats (duck, partridge, and game), various fishes, shellfish, snails, dairy products, eggs, wild greens, vegetables, other fruits (pears, plums, melons, and pomegranates), nuts (almonds, pistachios, and acorns), honey, spices, and seasonings.[34] Because these foods are only seen in small samples from disparate contexts, it is impossible to say what role each of these commodities played in the daily dietary regimen of a Neopalatial Cretan. We must also take into consideration social, religious, and environmental factors that might have influenced the production of these other foods. We can only say, therefore, that these things were present and eaten, but we are not able to understand their relative value or their place within the broader economy, palatial or otherwise. Moreover, as mentioned in the introduction, archaeobotanical samples are not created equal, and sample strategies, preservation quality, and research questions all affect the ways in which plant remains are reported in archaeological publications. Nevertheless, it is useful to think about the most ubiquitous agrarian products not obviously listed in the Linear A tablets, but frequently found in the archaeobotanical records.

One of the most striking results of archaeobotanical research at Neopalatial Cretan sites is that legumes are as commonly found as cereals and are often found together in the same contexts. In the Neopalatial period, legumes are present at twelve out of twenty-three sites. Within those twelve Neopalatial sites, five had grass pea/chickling vetch, four had lentils, four had peas, three had bitter vetch, two had broad bean, and one record had Cyprus vetch (Livarda & Kotzamani 2013: 14, fig. 9). In terms of specific Neopalatial contexts, legumes were present at one (out of one) building complex, one (out of one) medium/large settlement, three (out of ten) towns, four (out of four) villas, two (out of four) palatial sites, no burials, and one (out of one) cave site (Livarda & Kotzamani 2013: 15, fig. 10). Although the sample numbers are low, the pattern displayed here indicates that legumes were more common at lower-level or country sites (villas), rather than towns and

---

[34] Christakis 2008: 29. In addition, about fifty wild taxa have been identified in Neopalatial archaeobotanical records (Livarda & Kotzamani 2013: 20, fig. 14). These can be infiltrating weeds or plants purposefully cultivated. Examples include Poaceae and flax. For spices, only two coriander seeds have been reported (Livarda & Kotzamani 2013: fig. 12), but there is a presence of cumin-type starch grains at Sissi (Tsafou & García-Granero 2021: 13).

palaces.[35] Interestingly, Cyprus vetch (*Lathyrus ochrus*) is not found outside of Crete in Bronze Age contexts and might indicate local culinary traditions (Livarda & Kotzamani 2013: 13). Some of these legumes might be listed in Linear A records though are yet to be identified. Lentils, peas, and beans are good sources of protein and are not difficult to process. Other legumes, such as bitter vetch, are much more difficult to process for human consumption and might represent animal feed.

In contrast to macrobotanical studies, studies of microbotanical remains (e.g. chemical analyses of vessels and dental calculus) did not detect pulses in the starch assemblages from Neopalatial palace sites (Tsafou & García-Granero 2021: 12). This archaeobotanical absence, combined with their absence in Linear A records, might indicate that pulses were treated or valued differently than cereals. Stable isotope analyses from the LM II storage deposits from the Unexplored Mansion at Knossos, which is outside the palace itself, suggest that the production of pulses was household-based and not controlled by the palace, which might have been the case for cereals. Storeroom P has pulses (winged vetchling, Celtic bean), emmer wheat, hulled barley, and free-threshing wheat.[36] However, Neopalatial levels at the Palace of Malia have produced evidence for lentils, beans, peas, herbs, almonds, pears, and palm trees (Sarpaki 2007; Alberti et al. 2019: 55).[37] Many more systematic archaeobotanical studies are needed to fill out the picture of how the production of these various agricultural products was managed and to what degree they factored into a broader Minoan economy. As it stands now, the evidence seems to indicate that while these food products were commonly present, they were not consumed in large quantities, except for maybe certain legumes at specific levels of society.

3.2 Nonagricultural Goods

Though the chief focus here is domestic agricultural production, there are some indications that a few non-agricultural goods were produced in large numbers. It is unclear whether these goods functioned within the same type of cultural economy as the agricultural products. In the Linear A documents, perhaps the most prominent non-agricultural goods to be listed in substantial quantities are pottery and high-value finished objects. Two tablets from Hagia Triada (HT 31

---

[35] This is also the pattern seen with pulses. At a small house on the Lower Gypsades hill near Knossos only pulses were detected, again perhaps suggesting that these other types of starches were more important for lower social classes (Morgan 2015: 34–35). But see García-Granero et al. 2021 for the absence of pulses in microbotanical samples in cooking pots at Gypsades.

[36] Nitsch et al. 2019. Note, however, that the date is LM II, after the collapse of all the other Neopalatial court-centred buildings on the island.

[37] Sarpaki 2007.

and HT 39) record pottery. Large numbers (400, 300, and 3,000) following the vase-ideogram A 649 seem to suggest real vases.[38] This ideogram has been tentatively identified as conical cups (Schoep 2002: 188). Tripod and pithoi ideograms in the first section of HT 31 might also indicate real containers. However, it is not clear if these tablets are inventories of stock or book the incoming or outgoing movement of these containers. A pottery kiln dating to the Neopalatial occupation of Hagia Triada might suggest that pottery was being produced locally and that the tablets in question reflect the production of the site itself (Levi & Laviosa 1979–80: 7–47).

Unlike later Linear B texts, there are no extant inventories of raw material and/or finished objects recorded in the Linear A tablets. However, many specialized and high-value objects are found archaeologically and are often concentrated at palatial sites. For example, the "treasury" at Zakros contained various finished products, including ca. 50 stone vases and objects, faience rhyta, bronze double axes and tools, ivory inlays, and so on. In the ground floor room were found three ivory tusks, stone rhyta, bronze tools, six ingots, a silver vessel, and a gold ring (Platon 1971; Driessen & Macdonald 1997: 237). At Hagia Triada, Room 7 in the Villa contained five stacks of a total of nineteen bronze ingots, nine bronze statuettes, and gold foil. In addition, a bronze double axe and steatite cup were found in Room 57a (Halbherr et al. 1980: 123; Driessen & Macdonald 1997: 202–3). Despite the seeming abundance of raw material, especially bronze, there is no direct evidence of workshops at Hagia Triada. A possible reference to bronze is found on two tablets (HT 97.1 and HT 119.1), which list groups of people under occupational names. It has been suggested that A 327 could be the ideogram for bronze and on these tablets, it is followed by the quantities 33 and 34. This would be a reference to quite a large number of bronze workers (Schoep 2002: 189). However, this reading is not certain. That bronze should be accounted for in the Linear A records, along with pottery, makes sense within the context of a domestic economy focused on the production (and consumption) of agricultural goods. Bronze was necessary for the production of tools used in agrarian pursuits.

The mixture of finished products and raw materials found in palatial contexts might indicate that the palaces had some control over the acquisition and processing of high-value goods. The lack of direct evidence for workshops in these contexts, however, might indicate that the palaces acquired raw materials, and then sent them out to be processed, expecting the finished products to return in some manner. Indeed, the best evidence for craft production comes from

---

[38] On vases in the texts at Hagia Triada in general, see Montecchi 2019: 188–96.

larger towns.[39] This system might be a forerunner to the more formalized Linear B type of production called "talasia," see Section 4.4.2.

It should be emphasized, however, that most of the raw materials are imported (e.g. ivory, copper, tin, and silver) and so cannot be thought of as domestic products in the same way as grain, figs, wine, and so on. One could consider the finished objects as domestic products, but they would have likely been part of a separate, though slightly overlapping, economic network dealing in, specifically, high-status goods (see Murray 2023 in this series).

3.3 Neopalatial Systems for Production

Understanding Neopalatial systems of production and the role of Linear A documents hinges on our interpretation of the relationship between court-centered buildings, villas, towns, and rural communities. Indeed, most Linear A documents have been found outside court-centered buildings and our largest collection comes from a building normally classified as a "villa" (i.e. Hagia Triada).[40] These villas only start to appear during the Neopalatial period within particularly fertile regions and linked to major routes on the island. Essentially large farmsteads, villas vary in scale and context, but were often the central buildings of smaller settlements in the countryside. Examples of structures often called "villas" include Hagia Triada, Myrtos-Pyrgos, Nirou Chani, and Sklavokambos. To what degree the palaces controlled or merely interacted with these complexes is debated. They could be secondary administrative buildings directly connected to the larger palaces, or they could be residences of extended households or laborers used for the storage of crops, tools, and animals. Indeed, Militello et al. (2020) reconstruct an "imbedded production" at the villa of Hagia Triada where craft production extended beyond the needs of a single (elite) household and instead contributed to the larger local economy. The occupants are often viewed as emerging rural elites due to the scale and often elaborate construction of the main buildings. That systematic farming took place in connection with these structures is indicated by the archaeobotanical remains discovered there and through manipulation of the surrounding land-scape by means of dams and terracing (Haggis 2005: 76). We can see this happening throughout the island at this time, but especially in eastern Crete where it tends to be dryer (Flood & Soles 2014; Vokotopoulos et al. 2014). No matter what constitutes their exact connection to the palaces, these structures indicate an organization of labor above the household level.

---

[39]   For example, Mochlos (Soles 2003: 91–99, 2004) and Gournia (Watrous & Heimroth 2011: 205–6; Apostolaki 2014).

[40]   On the classification and characteristics of Hagia Triada, see Montecchi 2019: 309–12.

Archaeobotanical evidence suggests that villas produced the same types of staple agricultural products that are listed in Linear A tablets, alongside other edible plants. The archaeobotanical evidence from villas might therefore suggest that they not only specialized in the production of "palatial" goods, but also second-level products like legumes and pulses. The lack of large amounts of wheat, and especially free-threshing wheat, might suggest that villas produced these goods, but then shipped them to the palaces. Alternatively, the relative difficulty of producing free-threshing wheat might indicate that not all regions of Crete produced this particular grain.

Another indication that agricultural commodities and their derivatives were produced outside the palace and then brought in comes from evidence for perfumed oil manufacture. A 302 and its variants appear consistently in the Linear A tablets with common goods such as grain, olives, and wine. This suggests that plain and perfumed oil was habitually collected from and/or distributed to personnel in these Minoan centers (Palmer 1995: 145). Contexts in Linear A tablets versus Linear B present a pattern of management for olive oil very different from each other. Indeed, following the pattern for non-agricultural goods outlined previously, evidence for perfumed oil manufacture comes mainly from workshops in towns. It has been argued that Room 2.2 in Building C.7 at Mochlos was used as a perfumed oil workshop, as indicated by the types of equipment present and residues suggesting the use of olive oil alongside coriander and other spices (Brogan & Koh 2008). The control of resource production and transformation of secondary value-added products, such as perfumed oil and wine, suggests that rural communities were not passive providers of agricultural wealth but had their own agency and needs.

The scale and characteristics of storage facilities can help elucidate the relationships between central administration and production. Where surplus agricultural produce is stored and how much can be stored at one time could reflect systems of production. In general, pithoi (large clay pots) were the preferred method of longer-term storage, but it is likely baskets and sacks were also used, but not preserved in the archaeological record. Bins and below-ground silos are also attested at some sites. In his work on Minoan pithoi, Christakis (2008) concluded that most houses do not appear to have the storage capacity to cover annual requirements for the inhabitants. For example, at Malia, there is a relatively low storage capacity in the urban houses, which contrasts with the relative abundance of tools for processing agricultural produce (Christakis et al. 2019: 64). This trend appears to be the case for both the Protopalatial and Neopalatial periods. In other words, most Neopalatial houses did not have enough storage to be self-sufficient (Christakis 2008).

In contrast, the Protopalatial and Neopalatial palaces had both interior and exterior storage facilities that could store a large quantity of surplus foodstuff. At Knossos, the interior storage areas of the Neopalatial period had a total capacity of about 260,000 liters, 38 percent of which was used for cereals. According to Keßler's (2015: 148) calculations, 130–170 people could have been supplied for one year in the Protopalatial period, and this number increased to 170–220 people in Neopalatial period. At Phaistos, the Neopalatial palace had an internal capacity of between 34,500 and 40,100 liters – a yearly supply for about 22–34 inhabitants. Similarly, at Malia, the internal storage capacity of the First Palace would have totaled 12,700 liters, a yearly supply for only 8–10 people; while in Neopalatial times an overall volume of between 34,525 and 58,525 liters would have supplied 22–34 people for a year (Keßler 2015: 148). These calculations might therefore suggest that the *internal storage rooms* of the Minoan palaces were meant to secure their own self-sufficiency, if measured on a yearly basis (Keßler 2015: 161).[41] It is possible, however, that since these internal pithoi could be refilled, food was periodically brought in from the hinterland throughout the year. Certainly, the 97,720 liters of grain (AB 120) listed on a mixed commodity tablet from Hagia Triada would not fit inside the currently estimated internal storage facilities. It would require around 636 pithoi or four large silos, if those types of facilities existed at the time, whether inside the town or outside (Schoep 2002: 181). However, based on the existence of single-commodity tablets, it is clear the central administrators were nevertheless concerned with the acquisition of particular types of commodities in vast quantities, such as grain (AB 120), figs, olive oil, and wine. At Zakros, four complex single commodity tablets record wine and might indicate the palace's particular concern with controlling surplus production of that commodity.

How the central authorities acquired the products listed on single-commodity and totaling tablets is unclear. However, there is some indication that a few records might relate to assessments or taxes levied by the central authorities. The word KI-RO (sometimes abbreviated KI), in particular, might be related to a system of taxation (e.g. HT 123, 30, and 34) where KI-RO might mean something like "deficit" (Montecchi 2019: 108). In these contexts, the expected foodstuff might be provisions for large-scale feasts or religious festivals (Montecchi 2019: 205). However, mixed commodity tablets form the majority of Linear A texts, which suggests that in general the administrators combined information about goods and personnel according to the needs of the moment, rather than separating information into exclusive categories. According to

---

[41] See Keßler (2015: 160) on the external storage pits or *kouloures*, dated to the Protopalatial era at Phaistos, Mallia, and Knossos.

Palmer (1995), such a system might be considered "domanial" in that it is best suited to small-scale operation.[42]

Although the nature of record-keeping within Linear A administrative documents suggests central authorities did not exert an overabundance of control over agricultural production, the documents also make clear that there was a close relationship between the two sectors. Specifically, the central authorities were concerned with acquiring large amounts of grain, figs, olives, olive oil, and wine for various purposes. The large number of variants for the Linear A signs for grain, wine, and olive oil reinforce our impression of the local nature of the records. Administrators sensitive to the different qualities or types of these three products from one estate to another might make distinctions in the records, which is what we see in the Neopalatial period. That the variants might refer specifically to local distinctions of a particular commodity might be suggested by the fact that variants are often different at each site and rarely overlap. In contrast, administrators concerned with regularizing a system of recordkeeping and collection across wide areas (as in LM II-III Knossos) would be more likely to use generic ideograms (Palmer 1995: 146). In parallel with the idea of site-specific variants is the discovery that a high number of Linear A signs are also site-specific (Salgarella 2020: 155).

3.4 Minoan Palatial Summary

In conclusion, at the household or farmstead/villa level, Neopalatial Cretans were engaged in the production of a wide range of agricultural products from surplus subsistence goods, such as grain, to cultural commodities, such as olive oil and wine. Yet, at that level, they were also producing smaller quantities of legumes, pulses, and tubers, along with other herbs and plants. These extra-palatial entities also managed their own animals, though archaeologically it is difficult to reconstruct the scale of these activities. It is clear, however, that central authorities who used Linear A tablets to record their economic activities were not concerned with the governing of livestock. Instead, they were much more interested in acquiring large-scale surplus production of subsistence food including grain, figs, olives, olive oil, and wine. According to extant tablets, grain (AB 120) and figs were by far the most abundant commodities produced, whereas olives, olive oil, and wine were important but not collected on the same scale. Despite their incomplete view of the Neopalatial economy, Linear A tablets nevertheless indicate that palaces had particular interest in acquiring large amounts of specific commodities, but did not have as much to say about the means of production. However, tablets represent only one level of the extent

---

[42] Palmer uses the term "domanial" after Olivier (e.g. 1987).

administration, the other being represented by "sealing" administration.[43] The tablets themselves seem to be concerned mainly with different kinds of contributions, some of which are perhaps tax-based, as well as distributions either for services performed or to feed a dependent workforce.

4 Mycenaean Palatial Era

The Mycenaean Palatial Era encompasses the Late Helladic II and Late Helladic IIIA and B periods on the mainland and predominantly Late Minoan II and Late Minoan IIIA and B on Crete. In terms of absolute chronology, the Mycenaean palatial era spans roughly 400 years (ca. 1600–1200 BCE). During these periods, multiple phases of palatial buildings were constructed, but because the later palaces were built on top of the ruins of the earlier, we naturally know less about the earlier versions of these structures. While most scholars continue to use the term "palace" to discuss large central buildings of the Mycenaean era, they are very different from their Minoan counterparts. Instead of being built around open central courtyards, Mycenaean palaces have at their heart the "megaron" – a large reception hall with a central hearth and throne. Clues to the administration of these palaces are provided by clay tablets, sealings, and nodules on which were recorded various economic affairs.[44] Unlike the language of people living on Crete, however, Mainland people spoke an early form of Greek and the script in which it was written, Linear B, has been deciphered.[45] Consequently, scholars have been able to more or less definitively identify ideograms (pictures standing for words/ideas), numerals, and measures (both liquid and dry), along with any accompanying text.[46] Here, I follow others in equating one whole dry measurement to 96 liters and one whole liquid measurement to 28.8 liters.[45] Like Linear A, most of the identifiable ideograms are agricultural in nature and therefore help us to understand quantities of certain commodities and which resources were handled in specialized ways. However, unlike Linear A tablets, which have been found both inside and outside palace structures, Linear B tablets are mostly confined to palatial contexts. Several sites on the Greek mainland have produced Linear B tablets, but the vast majority are confined to Pylos, Thebes, and Mycenae.[47] On

---

[43] Schoep 2002: 189. The use of sealings and nodules within the Neopalatial administration is out of the scope of this particular work. For more information Hallager 1996; Palaima 1994.

[44] Here, I will focus mainly on the Linear B tablets as the major source of data for the same reasons I focused on Linear A tablets above. See note 16. For more on Linear B labels and nodules, see Del Freo 2024: 210–14.

[45] On the decipherment of Linear B, see Ventris 2024.

[46] On relative and absolute measures, see notes 17 and 18.

[47] Tablets have been found at a total of twenty-one sites on the mainland and Crete, but only eleven of those have administrative documents (see Salgarella 2020: 4, fig. 3). At the palatial complex of Ayios Vasileios in Laconia, over 100 tablets have been found, but are not fully published (Aravantinos & Vasilogamvrou 2012; Del Freo 2024: 221).

Crete, Linear B tablets are mainly found at Knossos and Chania.[48] Within these tablets, six agricultural commodities stand out for their high frequency and large quantity: grain (*120 and *121), figs (*30), olives (*122), olive oil (*130), wine (*131), and animals. Their derivatives, such as perfumed oil and textiles, also played a major role in production. The interpretation of Linear B texts and the meaning of specific entries for foodstuffs is greatly debated. Here, I will focus more on absolute numbers, to get a relative sense of how much of each commodity was represented and the relative proportion of one commodity versus another.

4.1 Agricultural Goods

4.1.1 Grain

Perhaps one of the most controversial topics in Linear B agricultural discussions is the identification of *120 and *121 as either wheat or barley. The traditional view since the era of Ventris and Chadwick (Palmer 1999: 16; Killen 2004), and upheld most recently by Halstead et al. (2022), is that *120 represents wheat and *121 represents barley (see also Killen 2004). That view has been challenged by Palmer (1992, 1995, 1999) and has gained support from others (e.g. Schoep 2002). In her most recent discussion of the topics, Palmer (2008) has maintained her view, but also concedes that the debate is not yet finalized and would only be finalized with the advent of new tablets or new archaeological contexts matching palaeobotanical remains with Linear B tablets, nodules, and so on bearing the corresponding ideogram. Because of this continual debate, I will here take the same approach as above for the Minoan era, and discuss both *120 and *121 under the same heading: "grain." Within this discussion, I will keep *120 and *121 separate so that future discoveries might indeed put definitive identifications to them and therefore draw more meaningful conclusions than here in relation to the relative production value of wheat and barley.

---

[48] The tablets found at Knossos form one of the largest collections of Linear B documents. However, not all documents date to the same time as the palace had suffered numerous conflagrations during the LM II-LM IIIB periods (unlike, e.g. Pylos, where the tablets seem mostly contemporary). There is great debate over which groups of tablets should be dated earlier or later. For an overview, see Salgarella 2020: 201–10; Olivier 2024: 76–78. Most agree with Driessen (e.g. 2008), that the tablets from the Room of the Chariot Tablets (RCT) are considerably earlier, and possibly dated to LM IIIA1 early. There is also some consensus that tablets from the North Entrance Passage (NEP) are later than the RCT, but earlier than the majority of tablets, and might represent an archive (Firth 1997: 58; Firth & Melena 2016; Salgarella 2020: 210; Driessen & Mouthuy 2022). Similarly, tablets from the Room of the Column Bases (RCB) are later than RCT but perhaps earlier than NEP and definitely earlier than the majority of tablets (Olivier 2024: 77). In addition there are other, small, groups of tablets that do not seem to fit, which indicates that other scattered tablets could date earlier (Olivier 2024: 78). In what follows, I attempt to account for the discrepancy in tablet groups when possible by separating out tablets from RCT, RCB, and NEP, specifically.

In her work on the topic of grain identification, Palmer (1992: 495, table 4) outlined the quantities of both *120 and *121 found on tablets from Knossos, Pylos, and Mycenae. According to her calculations, tablets from Knossos recorded a total of 1,468,603.2 liters of *120. The vast majority (over 1.3 million liters) come from contexts she labeled "collection of crops."[49] In contrast, only 3,333.6 liters of *121 were recorded, and only from contexts of rations and handouts. These are striking numbers, and a significant difference in quantities between the two commodities. *121 makes up only 0.23 percent of the total grain recorded at Knossos, which means *120 accounts for over 99 percent of the total grain. When compared to the Minoan palatial era, the tablets from Hagia Triada (where the most information exists) recorded 474,369.6+ liters of AB 120 and 7,968+ liters of A 303. The ratios are similarly disparate, with *120 and AB 120 recorded in significantly higher quantities than *121 or A 303 (which may or may not be the same commodity; see Palmer 1992, 2008). In this case, A 303 makes up 1.79 percent of the total grain, while AB 120 accounts for a little over 98 percent of the grain. It is hard to compare absolute numbers between the Minoan and Mycenaean eras since the records are not only different, but incomplete. If anything, it seems that the Mycenaean era on Crete continued the strong emphasis on grain, and specifically whichever grain is represented by *120 and AB 120.

However, the data presented by Palmer (1992: 495, table 4) includes tablets dating to different years and therefore need to be analyzed a little further. Because of the multiple conflagrations affecting the preservation of tablets at Knossos, certain groups of texts date earlier than the majority.[50] The homogeneity of texts from the NEP, and in particular groups I2 and I3, might suggest this area represents an archive (Salgarella 2020: 210). The chronology and contexts of these texts are particularly relevant to the calculations of *120 because the group of texts found in the NEP, and therefore dated earlier, contained sixteen tablets that recorded *120, eight of which record amounts over 100 units (E 777, 843, 849, 850, 1035; F 852, 853, 854) and one of which records at least 10,300 units (F 852). This one tablet alone, F 852, records at least 988,800 liters of grain harvest (*a-ma*) in hand (*e-pi-ke-re*) from the place *da-wo*, therefore accounting for just about two-thirds of Palmer's total grain count for Knossos (Killen 2024: 534). The remaining tablets from the NEP record around 2,000 units of *120, which equates to ca. 200,000 liters of grain.[51] Together, this only leaves around

---

[49] Palmer 1992: 493. "Collection of crops" total from: Tablets KN E 749, 843, 848, 971; E 845, 850, 1035, 8040; E 36, 71, 846, 4466, 5000, 132; and F157, F853, F851, F852, F854, 5001, 7050, 841.

[50] On this discussion, see note 48.

[51] Note that some of these texts record large quantities of *120 as rations (e.g. E 777), not harvests, but implies that the administration already has those quantities in hand in order to give them out and therefore could be considered part of a total quantity of grain available at a given time.

300,000 liters belonging to the majority of documents dating to later than the texts from NEP. This is not necessarily surprising given the different subjects of the later texts. That the vast majority of texts dealing with large amounts of grain were found in an archival deposit and dated to a time when the palace at Knossos was in full operation under a Linear B-using administration is expected and supports the idea that grain, and specifically *120, was the foundational aspect of the palatial agrarian economy from the earliest records to the latest. Interestingly, and in line with Palmer's observations, *121 is only recorded on one tablet from the NEP and in a small amount (just over 9 units).

At Pylos, a total of 33,340 liters of *120 were recorded, with the majority coming from rations and handouts. A total of 21,098.4 liters of *121 were recorded but with the majority in storage/inventory records rather than rations and handouts. The ratio between the two grains in this mainland context is very different from Knossos. Again, it is necessary to acknowledge potential differences in accounting and the location and survival of records. Nevertheless, the extant records from Pylos indicate a more even ratio between *120 and *121. *120 is still favored, but not in the same way we see on Crete. *120 accounts for 61.24 percent of the total grain, while *121 makes up the remaining 38.76 percent.

The Linear B records from Mycenae are few and relate to specific contexts, such as the Ivory Houses, rather than from record-keeping or storage rooms, as at Pylos. As a result, the extant records at Mycenae record significantly less volume of grain and, interestingly, with more *121. Specifically, 732.8 liters of *120 were recorded as rations and in uncertain contexts, while 866 liters of *121 were given as handouts and/or to religious personnel. No tablets represented collection records, which likely would have given a very different picture of the grain resources at Mycenae.

Overall, then, the Linear B records leave us with disparate views from each major palatial context. The tablets from Knossos suggest a continuation from the Minoan palatial era of a significant focus on *120, specifically. Even if Palmer's (1992: 495) calculation of around 1.5 million liters of grain is not exact, and does not take into account differences in time, deficits, and so on, it would not be off by more than half and that would still far exceed the amounts of *120 recorded at Pylos. Whether the significantly lower numbers at Pylos and the different ratio between *120 and *121 have more to do with tablet preservation rather than actual preferences or record-keeping strategies is impossible to know for certain. It is plausible, however, given the very different ecological contexts of central Crete and Messenia that these absolute numbers and ratios between the two grains could reflect actual differences in strategies between the two Mycenaean palaces.[52]

4.1.2 Figs

In Linear B texts, figs are most often represented by the sign *30, which can be used as a stand-alone ideogram (transcribed as *NI*) or syllabically as *ni*. Figs can also be indicated with the word *su-ko* (sometimes abbreviated to *su*). The word *su-za*, *sūtsai* (cf. Doric and Aeolic συκία), is associated with fig trees and can also be abbreviated by *su*. In form, *30 is very similar to its Linear A counterpart AB 30, which leaves little doubt to its identification.[52] Figs do not seem to be present on harvest or collection records and are most commonly associated with ration tablets, especially at Pylos (Palmer 1989; Killen 2004: 161, 2022). There, figs are always associated with *120 on rations given to female workers and children. Women receive Z 1.6 (9.64 liters) and children Z 0.8 (0.32 liters) every day. On tablet PY Fg 253, over 192 units of figs are listed and might equate to monthly rations for female workers. This amounts to approximately 18,400 liters or 22,080 kg (Hiller 1983: 196). A large quantity of figs is also recorded on KN F(2) 7346, which lists *NI* 612[or about 58,752 liters of dried figs (Killen 2004: 161). In addition to rations, figs show up on mixed commodity tablets as, perhaps, tithes from landholders (e.g. PY Un texts) and on records of food sent to shrines, usually in much smaller quantities (e.g. KN Fs series; KN F(2) 866: 10 units is unusually large; Palmer 1989: 102; Killen 2004: 162, table 8.4).

Large quantities of figs as produce can also be inferred from records of fig trees (Killen 2004, 2022). At Pylos, records of land include a reference to fig trees in association with grape vines. PY Er 880.6 lists 1,100 fig trees. According to Hiller's (1983: 196) calculations, that would equate to about 16,500 kg of dried figs (15 kg per tree). Similar numbers are recorded on tablets from Knossos. KN Gv 862.1, Gv 863.2, and Gv 864.2 record a total of at least 1,927 fig trees. There were likely more, however, since the numbers for the last two are incomplete. These fig trees would have produced at least 28,905 kg of dried fruit.

When compared to quantities listed in Linear A texts, figs seem to have remained a staple food, used in a variety of contexts, often alongside grain. Single large entries of figs are also similar to those listing *120 and show that the palaces were particularly concerned with the production of this nutritious and long-lasting staple commodity. The ubiquity and pervasiveness of figs is confirmed by archaeobotanical evidence. Fig plant remains are found in almost

---

[52] See Palaima 1992: 467–68 for a similar idea, but in the context of oxen use and agricultural production.

all palatial and non-palatial excavations where palaeobotanical research was conducted. At Tiryns, excavations produced 3,081 fig samples dated to LH IIIB, far outnumbering other foodstuff remains such as barley, wheat, and olive (Kroll 1984: 212). At Midea, an outstanding archaeological discovery of charred whole figs was found in the area of the West Gate in a storage context. Moreover, a clay sealing inscribed with *120 was found nearby and provides complementary archaeological evidence to the association of figs with grain in the Linear B texts (Margaritis et al. 2014: 273).

4.1.3 Olives

In Linear B, olives are represented by the ideogram *122 OLIV, and recorded by dry measurement. The syllabograms most commonly in ligature with the OLIV ideogram are TI and A, possibly representing different types of olives. TI could represent cultivated olives, while A represents wild (Melena 1983), or TI and A could be different qualities of oil (Foxhall 1995: 242). However, the former might be more plausible since olive oil had its own ideogram and remains of both wild and cultivated olives have been found archaeologically.

Quantities of olives recorded in Linear B tablets are quite large, rivaling figs in relative importance, and far outnumbering the quantities of olives recorded in the Linear A tablets (see Pratt 2021: 103–5, table 3.1). At Knossos, a total of 79,516.8 liters of olives are recorded. The vast majority derive from assessment or collection contexts. When accounting for differences in tablet group chronology, olives are relatively consistently reported. The earliest group from the RCT includes only two tablets with olive entries (F 157 and Uc 161). They record about 82 and 30 units (10,752 liters total), respectively, and from different contexts. The NEP tablets include three with olive entries (F 841 (46); F 844 (20 T2); and E 842 (24 T4)) totaling around 90 units or 8,540 liters. Therefore, while a few earlier tablets include olive entries, they do not make up the majority of olives recorded, in contrast to *120 and olive oil. This discrepancy is likely a result of the types of documents preserved during these different phases and perhaps the time of year the conflagrations occurred, particularly in the case of the "archive" at the NEP where grain is much better documented than any other commodity (except, perhaps, wine – see Section 4.1.5).

When compared to figs, olives are fewer in total quantity, but rival large entries like that on KN F(2) 7346, which lists *NI* 612[or about 58,752 liters of figs. Olives are recorded in much smaller quantities in Linear A tablets (e.g. Hagia Triada), but occupy a similar ratio to grain (AB 120) and figs (AB 30). The Linear B tablets at Knossos record about three-times as much of grain, figs, and olives, as the Linear A tablets at Hagia Triada.

At Pylos, a total of 11,892.9 liters of olives are recorded. The vast majority are in a deficits or inventory context. This means that the palace recorded quantities of olives that it expected to receive at some point and other quantities that it already has in storage. The total quantity at Pylos is far less than at Knossos, but similar in scale to quantities of figs and grain at this site. At Mycenae, tablets record 864 total liters of olives, all of which are recorded in an assessment or collection context. This may seem small, but when compared to entries of *120, it is comparable. Interestingly, at Thebes, 44,872 liters of olives are recorded. And, like Mycenae and Knossos, most can be found on assessment or collection tablets. However, in this case, the vast majority comes from a single tablet, TH Ft 140, that records an inventory of olive trees or an estimated harvest figure in five regions (Killen 1999: 217; Palmer 2008: 631, table 2). It is hard to interpret the Theban tablets or extrapolate information on olive production since the group of tablets is so specialized. However, even this one tablet indicates the palace at Thebes was interested in olive cultivation to a certain extent.

4.1.4 Olive Oil

In the Linear B tablets, olive oil is represented by the ideogram *130 OLE, and is recorded in liquid measurements. Liquid units reference a large container (VIN) that is probably the size of an amphora, not a pithos. The second size down from VIN is "S," which indicates a third of the large unit, VIN. The middle size, "V," is an eighteenth part of the liquid volume of a VIN and the smallest, "Z," is a seventy-second of the volume of a VIN (Bennett 2002: 80). Interestingly, olive oil is not modified by various descriptive ligatures as it is in Linear A. It is unclear why this discrepancy exists. It is clear that at least some Mycenaean palaces controlled the production of perfumed oil, best illustrated by the archaeological and textual remains at Pylos (Shelmerdine 1985; see Section 4.2.2). Perhaps this control over the production of perfumed oil within the palatial walls did not necessitate its collection from external sources, which might have been the case in the Minoan period on Crete.

Tablets from Knossos record a total of over 50,000 liters of olive oil. About half comes from deficit contexts while the remainder is split between assessment, religious offerings, industrial uses, and personal distributions. In terms of chronology, only one tablet from RCT records olive oil, but it includes two entries that add up to over 288 units, ca. 8,300 liters, though the context is hard to discern since the tablet is poorly preserved. Interestingly, the majority of olive oil entries comes from the Room of the Chariot Tablets (E1), generally dated to after RCT, but before NEP (Olivier 2024: 77). The total from the E1 Fh series tablets is at least 1,090 units, or about 31,000 liters of olive oil. One tablet alone (Fh 366 [+] 5,503) records just under 400 units or about 10,000 liters of olive oil collected from various villages (Godart 1968: 599; Killen 2024: 541). Other tablets written by the same hand (141) and dated to LM IIIA1 or IIIA2 within the Fh series (but not labeled as coming from E1) add up to 281 units or ca. 8,000 liters, putting the total olive oil from this chronological group at ca. 40,000 liters.[53] However, even when taking into consideration chronological differences, compared to the other commodities recorded in the tablets at Knossos, oil makes up a relatively small percentage of the total. It is less than half of the amount of olive fruit accounted for by the palace. One might consider that perhaps in some cases whole olives were brought in to be pressed at the palace, but no olive presses have been found in Mycenaean palatial contexts.[54] At Knossos, olive oil is found in almost every type of record, from assessments, to deficits, religious contexts (Bendall 2007a: 107, 110, 112–15), rations, payment, and a variety of industries including perfume production (3,000 liters), tanning, and bronze making. Olive oil was therefore a very versatile commodity but was not necessarily required in extremely large quantities. Even at Pylos, where perfume production is archaeologically attested, only a total of 1,623.6 liters of olive oil are recorded (Pratt 2021: 105, table 3.2). About 500 of those liters are allocated to perfume production. At Mycenae, only 86 liters of olive oil are recorded, despite the fact that the House of the Oil Merchant could hold between 2,700 and 3,600 liters of oil (Pratt 2021: 111, table 3.4). Although it is tempting to place a high value on perfumed oil and the production of it within Mycenaean palatial contexts, it only accounts for a very small percentage of the gross domestic production.

4.1.5 Wine

There are three ideograms for wine: *131a, *131b, and *131c. Palmer (1995) suggested that *131a is wine and *131b is vinegar because it is associated with perfume manufacture. However, there is no indication in any ancient source that perfume manufacture needed vinegar. Stanley (1999: 107) suggests instead that *131a refers to a superior wine, while *131b is an inferior wine that might have been produced from a second pressing of the grapes with added water. The ideogram *131c is a rare variation, detected in only three texts and two clay nodules. The nodules are from the Wine Magazine at Pylos. One of them has on

---

[53] Interestingly, no tablets recording olive oil were found in the NEP. Again, this could be due to preservation or the time of year the archive records.

[54] In LM III Crete, the most olive presses have been found at the coastal site of Kommos (Blitzer 1995).

its reverse a seal impression with the word "*e-ti-wa-no*." Stanley (1999: 108) interprets this to mean "genuine" (cf., Ventris & Chadwick 1973, έτανον) and so may be a designation of a particularly extraordinary vintage that needed to be authenticated. Wines could also have flavors or qualifiers, such as "honey," "sweet," and possibly indications of age (Stanley 1999; Pratt 2021: 115–16). In addition to the sign, the word *wo-no* (*woinos*, Mycenaean for "wine") is known from Pylos, tablet PY Vn 20. The word *wo-na-si* (*woinasi* "grapevines") occurs on Knossos tablet KN Gv 863 (Palmer 2002: 96). Interestingly, a tablet where the ideogram and the word for wine coexist has yet to be discovered (Palmer 1994: 28).

Tablets from Knossos record a total of 16,144.8 liters of wine. Here, the majority comes from assessment or collection tablets and a very small amount was used for religious purposes. Chronology plays a major role here, as it did with grain and olive oil. Only two tablets from the RCT record wine (Uc 160 (S5 V3 Z2); Uc 161 (60)), but the total is ca.1,700 liters. Much more significant is the single tablet from the NEP (I3), KN Gm 840, which alone records at least 498 units as payment (*a-pu-da-se-we*), equivalent to 14,342.4 liters. Palmer (2002: 103) suggests it might represent an amount collected for an entire district. Despite this one tablet, the total amount of wine recorded in the extant tablets at Knossos is surprisingly small considering how much of the other commodities. This is the case with the remainder of wine entries on later Fs series tablets where the quantities are only fractions of units, likely for regular religious disbursements alongside other commodities (total 20.8 liters; Pratt 2021: 106, table 3.3). The previous Linear A system on the island followed a similar trend, with wine usually present at sites, but recorded in smaller quantities. At Hagia Triada, out of the six commodities focused on here, wine is the least accounted for, other than A 303, which may or may not be a type of grain. This lack of wine at Knossos could be due to a number of factors. One could be the time of year these tablets were written, that is, before grape harvest season. However, that might not be an issue if the wine was produced in the countryside and then brought into the palace. It could also be that Knossos handled events differently than mainland palaces and did not necessitate storing wine collectively, but rather for one-time uses (hence why KN Gm 840 had such a large amount).

Tablets at Pylos record a total of 16,155.2 liters of wine. The majority comes from direct or indirect distribution records. This includes PY Vn 20, which records 410 units (11,808 liters) distributed to nine towns in the Hither Province. Unlike Knossos, wine makes up a lot more of the total agricultural goods collected here at Pylos. It is more comparable to the amounts of olives and figs collected and by no means stands out for its scarcity, as at Knossos. This greater focus on wine is emphasized by the Wine Magazine found at Pylos and the records of incoming wine shipments represented by clay sealings bearing the wine ideogram. The Wine Magazine at Pylos could store between 4,600 and 8,800 liters of wine. At Mycenae, only a total of 796.8 liters of wine were recorded in the context of assessment or collection. The number is small, but again, comparable to the other commodities listed above. Similarly, Thebes records 856.4 liters, but here in a religious offering context (Bendall 2007a: 161–63; Pratt 2021: 106–7, table 3.3).

4.1.6 Animals

The most frequently recorded and recognizable animals in the Linear B tablets are sheep (*106 OVIS), goats (*107 CAP(ra)), cattle (*109 BOS), and pigs (*108 SUS). Different ligatures and descriptions provide details about gender, types, and ages. Many other animals, including wild, are mentioned in the texts and found archaeologically, but should not be considered a large part of the economy (Halstead 1998–1999: 180–85; Halstead 2003; Fischer 2017: 215–97). The texts dealing with animals are generally divided between those dealing with livestock and the management of flocks/herds versus those dealing with the disbursement or delivery of animals to be eaten and/or sacrificed for religious and commensal purposes.[55]

Sheep are the most frequently recorded animals, especially at Knossos. There, about one-third of the ca. 4200 texts are about sheep and 80,000–100,000 sheep are recorded in the Knossian texts.[56] These sheep were kept in 590 flocks ranging in size from 30 to 400 head and distributed across central Crete where the palace seems to have entrusted wool flocks to named individuals on a yearly basis (Halstead 1998–1999: 154, 152–53, table 1; Isaakidou et al. 2019).[57] The palatial administration kept track of the number of animals, expecting the original number of sheep and their wool at the next inspection,

---

[55] The latter are sometimes termed "deadstock" in opposition of "livestock" (e.g. Halstead 2003; Halstead & Isaakidou 2017). The consumption records include a more even distribution of different species, whereas the livestock records focus predominantly on sheep (Halstead 1998–1999: 170).

[56] This number is restored from both complete and incomplete tablets. See Halstead 1998–1999: 154; Halstead & Isaakidou 2017: 120. This number increases to around 156,000 sheep when including 'inferred' and 'missing' sheep (Halstead 1998–1999: 159, table 2; Isaakidou et al. 2019: 37). The data concerning sheep flock management is predominantly housed in the Knossos D-series texts and mostly written by hand 117. Da-Dg lists flock distributions; Dn lists local totals of the same sheep; Dk are sheering records; Dl and Do record breeding ewes and lambs; and Dm lists male sheep at various locations (Halstead 1998–1999: 154–57).

[57] The number 590 also corresponds to the total possible shepherds listed by Olivier (1988). Some of the shepherd name entries are illegible, are debated, and are listed more than once (whether it is the same person or two shepherds with the same name is debated).

though they were not concerned with the age and sex of the returned sheep. Indeed, it has been argued that these herders took the liberty of culling old sheep and replacing them with sheep from their own herds.[58] About one-third of the sheep census tablets involve so-called "collectors," who were responsible for about one-third of the overall production (see e.g. Bennet 1992: 70–77, 86). Collectors are also seen on the KN Co series, which record mixed livestock in western Crete that probably belong to these individuals (Halstead 1998–1999: 157).[59] Certainly at Knossos, but perhaps also at other palaces, sheep played a major role in the economy predominantly for their wool (see Section 4.2.1). Goat records are less frequent at Knossos and the total number of animals recorded in extant texts (about 2,000) clearly distinguishes them from sheep in importance (Isaakidou et al. 2019: 37).

At Pylos, around 10,500 sheep (8,217 male) and 1,900 goats (1,004 male), are recorded on the extant tablets (Ventris & Chadwick 1973: 198; Halstead 1998–1999: 162–65, tables 3 and 4). One district, *pi-*82, counted 4,500 sheep. Since there are sixteen districts, although not all of them are the same size, the total at Pylos would come closer to Knossian totals (Hiller & Panagl 1976: 135 ff; Fischer 2017: 282). At Pylos 154 individuals are listed as responsible for flocks ranging from 10 to 230 animals, primarily sheep, but also goats and pigs. A single individual can herd multiple flocks. Interpretations of palatial involvement vary, but it seems that the flocks themselves are the property of or exclusively used by the palace (Killen 1993). Halstead (2001) suggests that shepherds could have their own flocks in addition to palatial flocks. The individual people listed were likely not actual herders in the field, but rather holders of the land on which the flocks were kept (Nakassis 2015: 593).

Compared to sheep, only a very small number of cattle are recorded on tablets from Knossos and Pylos. A total of around 370 cattle are listed on about 50 tablets at Knossos (Halstead 1998–1999: table 2). Interestingly, the majority of these tablets come from the earlier deposits in the RCT and especially the NEP. Groups of tablets dealing with cattle are predominantly in the C-series and include pairs of working oxen likely owned by the palaces and sent to subcenters (Palaima 1992; Halstead 2001). The names and/or descriptions of these oxen are included to differentiate individuals and keep track of their whereabouts, therefore preventing the return of different animals (Killen 1992–1993). The oxen pairs likely provided traction for the large-scale

---

[58] Halstead & Isaakidou 2017: 120–21. Breeding stock are also missing from the tablets, which might suggest that many animals destined for slaughter may have been raised outside of palatial administration (Halstead 2003: 258).

[59] The numbers of animals on these lists total preserved numbers add up to 2,849 sheep, 1,249 goats, 459 pigs, 26 cattle and a predominance of females (Halstead 1998–1999: 157).

grain production outlined in Section 4.1.1. This loaning of draught oxen was part of a "sharecropping" arrangement between the palace and nondependent farmers (Halstead 2001).

At Pylos, a much smaller number of cattle are recorded (about 30) on only eight tablets (Halstead 1998–1999: table 4). However, all eight tablets that refer to oxen directly seem to be very similar in nature, namely the contribution of animals for sacrifice (and consumption) at religious events (Palaima 1989; Godart 1999). A similar context appears to be recorded on some sealings from Thebes, which seem to be connected with the movement of animals from Euboea and outlying areas of Boeotia to the citadel of Thebes (Piteros et al. 1990: 153–55, 183–84 with references; Palaima 1992: 464). The only possible reference to oxen as draught pairs at Pylos is on PY Aq 64 and Aq 218. The "pairs" reference could be pairs of plough oxen, perhaps loaned by the palace as argued for Ch records at Knossos (Halstead 1998–1999: 168). The discrepancy between the types of tablets recording oxen at Pylos and Knossos might have to do with the time of year the texts refer to, or just an administrative difference (Palaima 1992: 472–73).

Unlike other animals, pigs seem to be exploited principally for their meat. On PY Cn 608, approximately nine towns list pigs to be fattened (SUS+SI). They are recorded as a calculated commodity according to the indirect assessment system, therefore moving from the districts to the palaces. At Pylos, pigs are mostly listed in quantities ranging from 2 to 57, but a total around 1,000 individuals. A few tablets stand out for their larger numbers including, PY Cc 665 with 190 pigs and PY Wp 1327 with 350. Most entries listing pigs list female pigs (eleven out of about twenty-five tablets). In stark contrast to their sheep records, the extant tablets at Knossos list about 375 pigs, the vast majority of which are female.[60] The tablets that list pigs are mostly from the earlier "archive" located at the NEP and provide quantities ranging from forty-one to eighty-seven.

In terms of the archaeological record, animals are perhaps one of the most easily detected categories of agricultural production. Zooarchaeological remains are very frequently found and analyzed at archaeological excavations. However, just like palaeobotanical evidence, there are many complications with not only data retrieval, but also analysis and publication.[61]

---

[60] For number of animals in the Linear B texts at Pylos, see Halstead 1998–1999: table 2. Note for pigs that he includes C 917 with an entry of 500, but the tablet does not record the ideogram SUS. The number could instead reference the female goats noted before the number, as it does for sheep in the line above.

[61] New analytical methods are currently being employed to understand nuances in animal subsistence and husbandry, such as multi-isotope analysis of tooth enamel (e.g. Isaakidou et al. 2019).

Furthermore, zooarchaeological remains predominantly record the remnants of meals (a.k.a. "deadstock" – animals intented for consumption), not the animals recorded in livestock texts (Halstead 1998–1999; Halstead 2003). However, we can still learn about aspects of animal use and consumption through their remains, especially when compared to the surviving texts. In his work doing just that, Halstead (1998–1999: 185) concludes that ". . . in decreasing order of certainty, surviving texts virtually ignore the widespread keeping of domestic dogs and consumption of numerous wild species, over-estimate the proportion of males among adult sheep and goats, and exaggerate the numerical predominance of sheep among the principal domesticates." Similarly, Isaakidou et al. (2019) used multi-isotope analysis of sheep and goat teeth enamel to conclude that the nuances of herding regimes apparent in the results are broadly in keeping with the documentary evidence in the Linear B texts at Knossos.

Although analysis of zooarchaeological remains from Pylos are not yet fully published, their initial investigation supports these statements and also points to specialized groups of deposits highlighting the importance of cattle at large-scale feasts. Six burnt bone groups from Pylos palace indicate specialized episodes of commensality. Each group contained at least five to eleven individuals totaling at least forty-six cattle and two deer (Isaakidou et al. 2002: 88; Halstead & Isaakidou 2004: 144, table 7). Halstead & Isaakidou (2004: 147) calculate that if several of the cattle were adult males, then each slaughtering episode may have fed between several hundred and several thousand guests. The type of meat and the scale of consumption might suggest that these deposits are remains of feasts for special occasions. Similar, specialized, deposits were found at Tsoungiza, a site about 10 km from Mycenae. There, a series of pits with tableware and faunal material were found. Halstead & Isaakidou (2017: 119) suggest that these pits are the remains of palatial feasts hosted by the nearby palace at Mycenae.

The most complete deposit from a palatial site that has been published fully is from Tiryns. Here, deposits span multiple chronological periods and allow for a long-term view of consumption. Interestingly, faunal assemblages at Tiryns suggest stable percentages of types of animals from LH IIIB to LH IIIC. These include ca. 30% sheep, 10% goat, 20% pig, and 35% cattle (Halstead 1998–1999: 173, table 5; Halstead & Isaakidou 2017: 121). Based on their work on zooarchaeological remains from multiple palatial sites, Halstead & Isaakidou (2017: 123) conclude that "commensality involving meat was a central concern of palatial . . . society."

4.1.7 Other Foodstuffs

There are many other agricultural goods mentioned in the Linear B tablets, some identifiable, others not yet connected to an ideogram. For example, the word for honey (*me-ri*) and its derivatives, is attested at Pylos, Knossos, and Chania. It is often recorded in small quantities and connected with religious texts (Bendall 2007a: 140–52; Varias García 2012). Based on context, honey was clearly an important product, but not one that was produced at the scale of the commodities discussed earlier.[62] One other cultivated product listed in the Linear B tablets that should be mentioned in the context of the Mycenaean economy is flax. Flax could be used for both its seeds (and resulting oil) and its fibers that were woven into linen textiles. Flax, as a cultivated plant, is designated by the syllabic sign *31* used logographically, and transcribed *SA*. It can also be indicated by the word *ri-no*, /*linon*/. It is attested at Pylos and Knossos in records related to fiscal matters. Since *SA* cannot be related to any Greek word indicating flax or linen, it is in general assumed that this is the abbreviation of an unknown non-Greek word (Del Freo et al. 2010: 344). Rougemont (2004) has argued that *SA* is used to indicate flax fibers at an early stage in the textile process, whereas *RI* stands for a later stage of the process when the fibers are ready for spinning or weaving. Interestingly, *SA* is used at both Pylos and Knossos in tablets dealing with land plots. The Mycenaean palace administration appears to have received a tax in kind on plots of land that were cultivated with flax (Foster 1981). In this case, *SA* is certainly identified as a cultivated plant by PY Na 520, which as the formula *pu -te-re ki-ti-je-si*, "the planters cultivate" (Del Freo et al. 2010: 344). However, most of the information related to flax is in the context of textile production (see Section 4.2.1).

In addition to the agricultural products listed in the Linear B tablets and outlined in the preceding sections, there are a few other plant species discovered archaeologically in Mycenaean contexts. Like the Minoan Neopalatial period, there are quite a few archaeobotanical assemblages of pulses, beans, vetches, and peas in both palatial and non-palatial contexts. These types of edible plants do not seem to be indicated in the Linear B records, even though they clearly played some role in the diet of Mycenaeans and their animals. At the palatial site of Midea, pulses are found usually all together in the samples and could have been grown as a maslin, or mixed crop. However, they were most likely used for human consumption because of their dense concentration as a clean product, stored and ready for cooking and consumption (Margaritis et al. 2014: 274). At Tiryns, bitter vetch was found (Halstead et al. 2022: 95) and in the Final Palatial

---

[62] In total out of the whole corpus on Linear B texts, honey is recorded forty times on thirty-four tablets (Varias García 2010: 406).

levels of Knossos' Unexplored Mansion, Celtic bean, Grass pea, and winged vetchling were found alongside free-threshing wheat and emmer wheat (Livarda & Kotzamani 2013). At the non-palatial sites of Kynos and Mitrou in Phthiotida north of Attica, bitter vetch, chickpea, Celtic bean, lentil, and grass pea were found alongside the cultivars listed in Linear B, such as einkorn wheat, emmer wheat, bread wheat, barley, olive, grape, and fig (Ntinou et al. 2022: 81).

4.2 Plant and Animal Derivatives

In addition to the primary agricultural products discussed thus far, a couple derivatives of those goods were also produced in large quantities and highly regulated by palatial authorities. Some of these goods might have functioned within the same type of cultural economy within which the primary agricultural products moved, but others seem to have been produced explicitly for their value as items for export. In the Linear B documents, the most prominent derivatives to be listed in substantial quantities are textiles and perfumed oil.

4.2.1 Textiles

The production of textiles occupied a significant portion of the extant palatial records. More than half of all Linear B tablets deal with textile production in terms of resources (flax and wool) and the monitoring of the palaces' textile workers and textile production (Nosch 2000a, 2012: 45). Indeed, at Knossos, close to 2,000 tablets are related to textile production. Certainly, most of the sheep recorded in texts described in Section 4.1.6 would have been used mainly for their wool, with meat as a secondary resource when old individuals were culled or on special occasions. The 100,000 sheep implied by the Knossos tablets would have procured 30–50 tons of wool for the palace (Halstead & Isaakidou 2017: 120). Wool itself is recorded by the ideogram *145 LANA. No direct noun for "wool" exists, but the adjective *we-we-e-a*, meaning "woolen," is recorded (KN L 178, 870). It is also possible that the ideogram LANA was used as a monogram for *ma-ru*, which might have been the Minoan word for wool.[63] The ideogram *145 can also be used as a quantity, the value of which is estimated to be 3 kg. Wool was not the only textile material, however. As mentioned earlier, flax was a common commodity in the records at Pylos and linen textile production is attested at both Pylos and Knossos.

Finished textiles themselves are also represented in the Linear B documents through a variety of ideograms and descriptions. The most frequent textile item is represented by the TELA ideogram (*159) and can be modified by endograms

---

[63] I thank an anonymous reviewer for this insight.

(syllabic signs written inside the ideograms), abbreviations, or adjectives.[64] TELA has the basic shape of a rectangle with small vertical strokes at the bottom that look like tassels. Adjectives describing TELA include *wa-na-ka-te-ra* or "royal." Other types of cloth include: *146, *166+WE, TUN+KI, TUN +RI, *ki-to*, and *pa-we-a* (for a list of all ideograms related to wool/flax and textiles see Del Freo et al. 2010: 340, figure 17.2). Finished textile products can be described by their color and additions, such as fringes.

That palaces were concerned with the production of textiles themselves is also clear from the tablets dealing with various professionals involved in different stages of production such as combers, spinners, fullers, weavers, seamstresses or tailors, and so on. (Del Freo et al. 2010: 345). Textile techniques, textile occupational designations, and textile types are identical from one palace to another. However, palaces seem to have differed in the way that the production of cloth was handled by palatial authorities and how much control was exerted over various individuals and their outputs.

At Knossos, textiles were produced in a decentralized industry. Workers were scattered in different towns but reported directly to the palace. As mentioned earlier, nearly 2,000 tablets concern textile production. Records in D, L, and Od series are involved with the textile industry and specifically herds of sheep and their wool production. Records in Ak and Ap series record details of groups of women and children involved with textile manufacture using allocations of raw materials from the central authorities. Lc tablets record targets for production which were set for the groups. Le series record the final receipt by the palace of the finished products (Killen 1984: 50–51). Ak tablets list a total of 500+ women but more likely upwards of 1,000 workers; also about 200 male textile workers (Killen 1984: 52). These workers were located not in the palace itself, but in various towns in central Crete.

In contrast, Pylos' textile industry was organized similarly, but much more centralized. Although, the records are incomplete and less numerous, it is nevertheless possible to reconstruct a basic production model. Records in Cn series deal with sheep flocks. Aa and Ab series at Pylos record women and children textile workers who likely fully dependent and were maintained by the palace on a full-time basis. There are around 600 women listed on Aa tablets (Killen 1984: 52). The centrality of the Pylos industry is indicated by the majority of the workers located at Pylos and Leuktron, the major center in the Further Province (Killen 1984: 55–57). One other location in the Hither Province, *ro-u-so*, seems to have been important for textile production, and

---

[64] One adjective might describe textiles produced or designated for export: *ke-se-nu(ne)-wi-ja* attested in the Knossos Ld 573, Ld 574, Ld 585, and Ld 649 tablets qualifying cloaks (*pa-we-a*) and textiles (TELA). See Nosch 2014; Killen 1964: 14; Tzachili 2001: 169–71.

specifically finishing and decorating (Killen 1984: 60). Another important contrast between Knossos and Pylos is the latter's emphasis on linen production and the procurement of cloth through taxation. Around 100 tablets record flax in the Na series and 530 pieces of *wehanos* *146 are expected in the Ma taxation records (Nosch 2012: 46; Killen 1984: 53). However, *146 might not always designate cloth made from linen (Nosch & Perna 2001: 471–77). This is the one variety of cloth that was supplied as a finished product to the center by way of taxation payments and not directly under the oversight of the palace.

4.2.2 Perfumed Oil

Perfumed oil was a product common to many cultures of the Bronze Age Mediterranean (Fappas 2008). It should come as no surprise, then, that Mycenaean palaces were also concerned with the production of specialized oils. In the Linear B tablets perfumed oil had two forms: a more liquid one (OLE which signifies oil) and a thicker unguent type (AREPA; Shelmerdine 1985: 31). Most of our textual data about perfumed oil comes from Pylos, where the extant texts indicate concentrated palatial interest in the production of various perfumed oils with ingredients such as coriander, cyperus, and henna, which might have been used to dye the oil.[65] The archaeological record corroborates these data in the form of an excavated perfume workshop inside the palace itself. However, it is also possible that the palace at Pylos regulated external perfume workshops at other locations. Palaima (2014) interprets tablet PY Vn 130 as a record of the status of unguent-boiling operations under the control of a man named Kessandros throughout the nine districts of the Hither Province at the time the text was written. The palatial administration here is concerned with containers and wood supplies that were used to do the actual perfume making, not the aromatics and other materials as on PY Un 267. It suggests a division of responsibilities with a man named *a-ko-so-ta* in charge of perfume ingredients on PY Un 267 and *ke-sa-do-ro* with vessels and fuel on PY Vn 130. Also, two individuals identifiable from other tablets as *qa-si-re-we* (local-level administrators of manufacture/crafts) are mentioned in PY Vn 130 as involved in seeing to the practical details of perfume making in specific localities. So, the palace is working with other officials to assist in particular activities, maybe in an irregular or ad-hoc way. In this way, perfume production does not seem to fall into the group of activities regulated by the *ta-ra-si-ja* or "*talasia*" system where palaces give manufacturers raw materials, such as bronze, and expect finished products in return (Killen 2001: 169–72; see also Section 4.4.2).

---

[65] But see Foster 1977 for perfume at Knossos. For ingredients, see AN 616 r, Un 249, Un 267, and Un 592 kept in Archive room 7–8; Shelmerdine 1985: 8, 17–23, 151.

Other evidence for the manufacture of surplus perfumed oil comes from evidence for its storage. Room 23 at Pylos has been identified both as a storage area for perfumed oil (with embedded pithoi) and as a scribal center for recording its disbursement (Blegen & Rawson 1966: 136, fig. 3.3; Shelmerdine 1985: 87–88). An adjacent room, Room 24, also seems to have functioned as an oil storeroom with large pithoi in benches around the wall and a sealing (Wr 1437) with the word AREPA inscribed on it (Shelmerdine 1985: 88). Rooms 32 and 38 may have also been storerooms associated with perfumed oil, as posited by the original excavators (Blegen & Rawson 1966: 156–60, 170–73).

Actual quantities of perfumed oil used in palatial contexts are listed in tablets related to feasting and offerings to deities. The quantities of perfume for consumption at commensal events as recorded in Linear B tablets (Un 6, Un 718, Un 853, and Un 1177), while insufficient for distribution to all the estimated participants, were nevertheless prodigious (approximately 24 liters; Murphy 2012: 257). In addition, Bendall (2001: 260) argues that at least 86 percent of the Linear B Fr disbursement tablets refer to perfumed oils in religious contexts and several of these are feasting activities.[66] Often the individual deities are named as the receivers of these gifts of oil. The adjective "Potnian" (PY Un 249) was used to describe a perfumer, as well as the perfume intended for the goddess (Shelmerdine 1985: 20; Lupack 2007: 56). Potnia also received perfumed oil "for (the pieces) of *wehanos* cloth, as ointment" (*we-a$_2$-no-i a-ro-pa*; PY Fr 1225; Nosch & Perna 2001: 475, 477). A variation of this goddess, the Potnia *Aswiya (*a-si-wi-ja*), perhaps a foreign deity, was "owed" (*to-so qe-te-jo*) a large amount, 5 V4 (ca. 150 liters), of sage-scented perfumed oil on PY Fr 1206 (Morris 2001: 424). Bendall (2014) argues that this large amount on tablet Fr 1206 was given to Potnia *Aswiya as a one-time (or once a year?) gift and shipped to her sanctuary in Anatolia. A different goddess, the "Divine Mother" (*ma-te-re te-i-ja*) was also given a similarly large quantity (5 S1 or 153.6 liters) of sage-scented oil on PY Fr 1202. Unlike the gift to Potnia Aswiya, this does not seem to be an annual gift since a single month or festival (*me-tu-wo ne-wo*; the "New Wine") is specified (Morris 2001: 424).

The production of surplus perfumed oil seems to have had different purposes within different palatial contexts. None of the extant Linear B tablets discuss the export of perfumed oil in exchange for other commodities. For the perfumed oil production industry at Pylos, none of their locally-made containers have been found abroad. This could be an indication that palatial perfumed oil production was limited to local use and exchange. At Mycenae, however, there is more of

---

[66] However, it is not entirely clear exactly how perfumed oil was used at feasts. See Fappas (2008: 369–73) for suggestions.

an indication that surplus perfumed oil was produced in order to be used on an external exchange network (Palaima 1991; Fappas 2008). Specifically, the circulation of small decorated closed containers (stirrup jars, alabastra, and flasks), most often used for perfumed oils and unguents, might work as a proxy for the commodity itself. For example, out of a total of 206 imported Mycenaean vessels found in the tombs at Ugarit, 101 were closed vessels (stirrup jars, piriform jars, alabastra, and flasks; van Wijngaarden 2002: 288). At the site of Enkomi on Cyprus, mortuary contexts produced 973 imported Mycenaean ceramics, of which 426 were small closed vessels (van Wijngaarden 2002: 296).[67] As discussed in what follows, most of those vessels found on Cyprus and the Levant originated in the Argolid.

4.3 Non-agricultural Goods

Finally, some non-agricultural goods were imbedded in Mycenaean systems of production. However, the ways in which they were regulated by palatial administration seem to differ from other products and might have employed specialized methods of interacting with artisans and producers. Here, I will focus on pottery production and the use of metals and other exotic materials to produce high-value items.

4.3.1 Pottery

Although few Linear B documents mention pottery or potters, it is clear from archaeological material that the production of pottery was an important component of local and palatial, and economic life. It was used in every household, but it was also used as an integral part of regulated consumption practices and intercultural trade. To give some indication of scale, over 8,540 ceramic vessels were stored within the Pylos palace complex at the time it was destroyed (Whitelaw 2001: 52). Most of these were for producing and consuming food and drink. Some, however, were industrial or used for storing or transporting goods. Whitelaw (2001: 62–64) estimates the palace to have had an annual consumption of around 12,000 vessels, but the population within the palace's province consumed between 37,000 and 75,000 pots. If this is expanded to the whole kingdom, 612,000–1,255,000 pots would have been needed per year. These numbers suggest that the palace was not necessarily the driving force behind production of ceramics. In fact, the palace's ceramic needs could be fulfilled by one or two full-time potters. In contrast, the polity would have required 450–500 part-time potters, one to four per village. Therefore, it seems

---

[67] The high value of these vessels and their contents can also be indicated by the production of local imitations; e.g. at Ugarit (Mattoïan 2004).

that most pottery was likely produced locally, but that the palace required a certain quota, which it ensured was filled, by means of controlling specialized workers. For example, the Linear B tablets at Pylos identify four potters (*ke-ra-me-u; ke-ra-me-ja*; Hruby 2011), one of which is labeled "royal" (*wa-na-ka-te-ro*) and appears in land-holding tablets along with administrators and craftspeople (Whitelaw 2001: 71; Hruby 2013: 423). It is perhaps not coincidental that about half of the pottery from the palace was produced by the same potter (Hruby 2013: 424).

In terms of the types of vessels Mycenean palaces were concerned with, thirteen vessel names appear on the tablets at Pylos including hydria, tripod, amphora, phiale, and depas cup (Hruby 2010: 201). There are also a few tablets dealing with the acquisition of pottery. Two tablets from Knossos list 900 (K 700) and 180 (K 778) large stirrup jars.[68] In some locations, such as the Argolid, specialized pots including decorated stirrup jars and kraters, seem to have been produced specifically for an eastern export market (Jung 2021: 151). At least 7,000 LH IIIA2-B vessels of Mycenean manufacture have been identified at numerous sites in Cyprus, the Levant, and Egypt, as well as along the western coast of Anatolia and Italy (see Van Wijngaarden 2002; Murray 2017: 191, table 4.4; Murray 2023: 38).

4.3.2 Metals and High-Value Objects

Unlike the Linear A tablets, Linear B tablets recorded the production of high-value objects. It should be emphasized, however, that most of the raw materials were imported (e.g. bronze) and so cannot be thought of as domestic products in the same way as grain, figs, wine, and so on.[69] One could consider the finished objects as domestic products, but they would have likely been part of a separate, though slightly overlapping, economic network dealing in, specifically, high-status goods (see Murray 2023 in this series).[70] The most prominent imported resource that was then distributed for manufacturing was bronze. For example, at Pylos, the Jn series of Linear B tablets as a whole records from 594 to 1,046 kg total of bronze and about 270 bronze-smiths (Killen 2001: 173; Nakassis 2015: 591, n. 32).[71] As discussed in Section 4.4.2, bronze was part

---

[68] On transport stirrup jars and their implications for Mycenaean administration and economy, see Pratt 2016 and references therein.

[69] However, there is some indication that silver was mined and exported in Greece (Sherratt 1993, Wood et al. 2021).

[70] This could be thought of like the advertising on Triscuit brand crackers: "Proudly grown & baked in the USA with globally sourced oil and salt" (note the " . . . with globally sourced oil and salt" is in much smaller font).

[71] 594 kg represents the minimum amount of bronze distributed in the Jn series without duplicating amounts from "working tablets" as defined by Smith 1992–93. 1,046 kg is the amount of bronze

of the *talasiā* system where raw materials were distributed under palatial control and finished products, such as chariots and weapons, were collected. In general, inventories of metal vessels that were to remain within the palace at Pylos are highly detailed and describe workmanship, decoration, condition, number of handles, and other characteristics (Hruby 2013: 426). Other imported raw materials used in the fashioning of local products include alum (PY An 35.5–6; Perna 2005), gold (PY Tn 316), blue glass, and ivory (PY Va 482); however, the tablets mostly list finished products or workers, not the means by which the materials were acquired or produced (gold worker: *ku-ru-su-wo-ko*; blue glass worker: *ku-wa-no-wo-ko*; Bennet 2008). One exception could be ivory-working. Tablet PY Va 482 might list a pair of ivory tusks being supplied to an ivory worker with a note on the types of objects expected in return (Killen 2015: 846). Archaeologically, the remains of workshops dealing with these imported raw materials are usually found within the palaces themselves.

Finally, there is new evidence for the presence of another local natural resource that could have been a high-value product of Mycenaean Greece: lignite (a.k.a. brown coal). Work by Buckley et al. (2021) has identified lignite in dental calculus at Tiryns suggesting the use of coal for a fuel source. Moreover, the lignite was identified as having come from deposits near Olympia, implying a network of coal extraction and distribution during the Mycenaean palatial era.[72] The extent to which lignite was mined is uncertain, but it could have been instrumental in the production of other objects, such as metalworking and ceramic kilns. Interestingly, the research team did not find lignite residue on other individuals from the Levant and Egypt, which might imply it was a product of Mycenaean Greece, specifically, and could have been another high-value commodity in and of itself.

4.4 Mycenaean Systems of Production

How the Mycenaean palatial states regulated production of the above agricultural and non-agricultural goods was eclectic. Based on evidence from the Linear B tablets, there seems to have been at least five systems of production, some of which overlapped with each other for certain types of goods. While most of our information comes from Pylos and Knossos, there does seem to be a fair amount of consistency with the types of systems in place; however, their

---

recorded on the totaling tablet Ja 749. The restored number of bronze-smiths is about 400 (Killen 2001: 173).

[72] Indeed, there are vast lignite mining operations still ongoing near the modern city of Megalopolis in the Peloponnese. The deposits throughout the region are surface deposits mined as opencast resources, which would have made them visible to ancient populations (i.e. they would not have needed to go deep underground; Buckley et al. 2021: 3).

exact execution did vary from palace to palace. This variation is likely due to each palace's specialization in certain commodities based on available natural resources (e.g. flax at Pylos) and traditional resource production over time (e.g. wool at Knossos). Production of goods considered important to the palaces could be extracted from others under the auspices of the palace or directly controlled by palatial authorities. It should be noted, however, that not all goods were controlled or extracted by the palace and the palace represented only one (large) node on a much larger economic network. The gaps left by the Linear B tablets can be as informative as the details contained therein. We can therefore only see hints at specifically palatial systems of production used to extract only the resources listed on the tablets themselves (Bennet & Halstead 2014). As discussed earlier, there seem to have been many other resources, such as various legumes, that are not discussed in the tablets but formed a part of the agricultural goods produced and used in domestic and palatial contexts.

4.4.1 Taxes and Assessments

The Linear B documents indicate that there was both a direct and indirect assessment system for the collection of agricultural commodities. Both systems were based on detailed surveys of crops and animals throughout the kingdom, from which estimated production could be calculated. Tablets with entries related to an individual flock, plot of land, or person were recording the direct assessment. Amounts will often be irregular and connected to places closer to the palace center (Palmer 1989: 181). For example, staple grain production and collection were concentrated around major centers (Bennet 1985: 246; Killen 1992–1993, 1998). Indirect assessment or portioning relates to a region's capacity for production. Once the central administration calculates this potential yield for a specific region, it sets a total target figure for the kingdom and divides that up based on a region's capacity. Indirect assessment tablets list places or groups some distance away from the palace center. In both of these categories, the production unit can be as large as a whole district, as with the Ma series (Shelmerdine 1973; Killen 2008), or it can be as small as one smith out of a group, as in the Jn *ta-ra-si-ja* tablets.

Assessments like these can be considered similar to taxes (Shelmerdine 1988). The Pylos Na series records taxes to be paid in flax, which was directly related to landholdings (Ventris & Chadwick 1973: 469–71; Killen 2008: 170). For example, the high-ranking "collector" (see Section 4.4.5 named **we-da-ne-u* was responsible for furnishing twenty rowers (An 610.14) and his landholding in the Na series corresponds to a total of twenty units of flax (Na 856, Na 1041). Other tablets are not related to landholdings, but to taxation through the supply of finished products. The Pylos Ma tablets show that one type of textile, *146, was acquired through taxation payments from various subordinate districts of the kingdom (Shelmerdine 1973, 1988).

4.4.2 The ta-ra-si-ja *(talasiā) System*

In the Linear B tablets at both Knossos and Pylos, there is a system of production labeled *ta-ra-si-ja* (transliterated as *talasiā*), which is best translated as "an amount [of raw material] weighted out and issued for processing" (Ventris & Chadwick 1973: 583; Killen 2001: 161).[73] This system falls under the category of indirect assessment and was mainly used for the production of luxury items or items requiring specialized labor and knowledge to produce. These included bronze objects, such as chariots and weapons, and various types of textiles. In this system, the palace would supply raw materials, such as wool and bronze, to workers who would then produce the items and return them to the palace. The exact relationship between the workers and the palaces is debated and suggestions range from fully dependent, to independent but lower status, or independent artisans (Killen 2001: 175; Duhoux 2008: 268). In addition, these workers are spatially distributed throughout the kingdom and likely received allocations on a yearly basis (Killen 2001; Nosch 2006; Nakassis 2015).

The great majority of the cloth in which the palaces at Knossos and Pylos had an interest was produced under the *ta-ra-si-ja* system. This involved the palace supplying wool to various workers, from whom the center would expect in due course to receive an equivalent quantity of finished fabric (Killen 1984: 61; Killen 2000; Nosch 2000b). As discussed earlier under "Textiles (Section 4.2.1)," the palaces had different means of acquiring the raw wool material and its production was highly regulated by palatial interests, though distributed widely throughout the kingdom (Godart 1977). In the case of textiles, everything is handled locally, from management of flocks to sheering of wool and production of textiles. Only the finished product makes its way to the palace. The palace, however, records all the information concerning these activities despite not being directly in control. In contrast, bronze was acquired through external channels by the palaces, but distributed using the *talasiā* system in order to produce finished goods. Smiths (Linear B *ka-ke-u, khalkeus*) were a heterogeneous group that included members of the elite (Nakassis 2013: 74–102). At Pylos, 225 named individuals are listed as smiths who receive various amounts of bronze, usually a few kilograms. It is interesting that many of these people

---

[73] The word *ta-ra-si-ja* might be related to the later Classical word *talasía*, which corresponds to *talanton*, a Classical unit of measure equivalent to c. 25.8 kg (Ventris & Chadwick 1973: 56; Killen 2001). For more on the talasia system, see Nosch 2006, Montecchi 2012.

are listed as doing other jobs or maintaining other aspects of palatially interested production. It is unlikely that each one of these individuals was themselves a bronzesmith with the knowledge and equipment (i.e. forge) to produce high-level objects. Rather, these could represent people to whom the palace entrusted raw bronze who then brought the bronze to the nearest smith for the production of tools and weapons. If the same people are managing farms and giving a specific amount of produce to the palace, then bronze would be necessary for the production of tools. The allocation of bronze could have been another way the palatial administration managed and held power over other people.

4.4.3 Land Registers/Cadastral Survey

Another way that the palaces seem to have had control over at least some direct production is through land allocation and ownership. However, there has been a general consensus lately that, although the palaces did control some choice pieces of land, which they doled out accordingly, they did not own outright the vast stretches of land needed to produce the large quantities of goods recorded in the tablets (see references in Bennet & Halstead 2014). The palaces may have relied upon non-palatial landowners in the surrounding kingdoms (Palmer 2001: 60). For example, a tablet from Pylos (Un 718) records wine delivered from four separate donors. The wine is in varying amounts, but the total is roughly 153.6 liters. Interestingly, wine is the only commodity all four people provide, suggesting that all of their estates included vineyards. In addition, the fifty record-keeping nodules recovered from the Wine Magazine at Pylos included thirty-three individual seals, supporting the hypothesis that the seals belonged to the wine producers, rather than to officials collecting the wine (Palmer 1994: 163). That these landowners produced multiple products is indicated on the reverse of a tablet from Mycenae (Ue 611) that records a delivery of commodities by a single person including two kinds of olives, figs, and wine (Palmer 2002: 99). At Knossos, a tablet, F(2) 845, might indicate collective wheat fields and olive groves. This tablet records "*da-mo*" olives contributed to palatial stores, which might indicate these crops were produced on *damos* land where *damos* means something like "village community" (Killen 1998: 20). Alternatively, *da-mo* here could reference "separate estates owned and managed by the central power" (Halstead 1995: 18). Whether this applies to all the tablets of this variety or if this tablet is distinguished from the others by listing it as from *da-mo* land is impossible to know (Killen 1998). It is clear, however, that outside landowners were in no way independent from the palaces. Wine and fig producers in particular seem to have been an object of concern for the palatial administration since there is a special title for the individual in charge of collecting tithes, contributions, or taxes from these independent vineyard and orchard owners: *o-pi-ka-pe-e-we* "overseer of vines" listed on PY Jn 829 and *o-pi-su-ko* 'overseer of figs'.

Some tablets, however, indicate the palace did have some control over choice pieces of land and their products. For example, two totaling tablets (*a-pu-do-si*) of oil contributions to the Knossos Palace (tablets Fh 366+5503 and Fh 367 +5460) list 10,171.66 and 9,900 liters, respectively. This amount of oil production would correspond to around 4,000 trees and 3,960 trees (Melena 1983: 105). Keeping in mind that this calculation is based on only two tablets, we must assume that the actual amounts were far greater. That the palace was at least concerned with some vineyards is made apparent by Knossos tablet Gv 863, which may describe two different methods of raising vines at a location very near to the palace, *qa-ra* in Linear B. The first line has the word *wo-na-si*, a locative plural form of *woinades* "grapevines." On the second line, vines are called *we-je-we*, *huiewes*, meaning vines that are trained to climb up trees (Palmer 1994: 59–60). Palmer suggests that the ideogram after these words describes the age of the vine (Palmer 2002: 99). This one tablet implies that palatial central authorities had some influence on decisions pertaining to these two highly sophisticated methods for optimal vine growth. The notation of the age of the vines is a surprising detail that also hints at the intensity with which the palaces regulated vineyards, and presumably their produce. In addition, the Knossos Gv tablets refer exclusively to vines and fig trees. Specifically, tablet KN Gv 862 mentions 1,770, 405, 10, and 17 fig trees, then 20 and 225 vines. Tablet KN Gv 863 lists 420 vines and 104 fig trees; KN Gv 864 lists 69 vines, 53 fig trees, and another (illegible) number of vines (Platon & Kopaka 1993: 93). The two species are in new combinations at Pylos in tablet PY Er 880 where 1,100 vines (*we-je*) are followed by 1,100 fig trees (*su-za*). These Knossos and Pylos tablets may indeed refer to the strategy of growing grapevines up trees, and in this case, fig trees.

4.4.4 Oxen Leasing

There is some indication that Mycenaean palaces might have controlled the production and collection of agricultural goods through controlling the means of production in the form of plow oxen and human labor. Paul Halstead's (1999, 2007) work on wheat, flax, and cattle hypothesizes that the Mycenaean palaces loaned expensive cattle to farmers during plowing season and personnel during the reaping season.[74] In return, the palaces received a certain share of the

---

[74] For the oxen tablets, including the KN Ch tablets naming individual animals (e.g. Killen 1992–1993), see Section 4.1.6.

finished product. Specifically, the harvest tablets from Knossos and the E-series land registers from Pylos show share-cropping arrangements between the palaces and the *da-mo*, where the *da-mo* provided the labor and the land and the palace supplied ox teams and fodder (see also 1998). In the case of olives and vines, we might speculate that the central authorities may have mobilized the labor needed to harvest fruit, as well as control the equipment and knowledge for the production of the oil and wine.

4.4.5 Overseers

One of the most complex systems of production involved a group of people referred to as "collectors" who seem to have been organizers of various industries and procurers of raw materials, such as wool from palatial flocks (Rougemont 2009: 249–524). Only four individuals at Pylos are named as collectors. However, these individuals had many jobs and were generally higher-ranking individuals within society. Nakassis (2015: 589) suggests we think of Mycenaean collectors not as a coherent group of administrators, "but as members of a wider group, namely supervisors identified by personal name." For example, in his work on individuals within the Linear B texts at Pylos, Nakassis singles out a collector named Aklsoitās (Linear B *a-ko-so-ta*) who also appears fifteen times in shepherding texts, supervises a land inspection, and acts as an agent that gives, receives, and distributes various goods (Nakassis 2006: 385–86).

There were also individuals who received titles appropriate to their jobs, such as *o-pi-su-ko* 'overseer of figs' and *o-pi-ka-pe-e-we* 'overseers of vines' listed on PY Jn 829. These titles were listed along with the provincial officials *ko-re-te*, *po-ro-ko-re-te*, and *du-ma-te*, suggesting that the provincial administrative network included individuals specifically concerned with figs and vines. Their jobs might have included assessment and collection of these crops throughout both provinces (Palmer 1989: 180, 1994: 64). In the same category of overseers are individuals who supervised work groups. These named individuals were responsible for a group of workers processing or producing various goods. For example, at Pylos, work groups called *qa-si-re-wi-ja* (*gasilēwiā*) and *ke-ro-si-ja* (*geronsiā*) are always accompanied by a personal name in the genitive, indicating the supervisor of the group. On tablet Py An 340, thirteen named individuals are managed by a man named *a-ta-o* in the context of craft production (Nakassis 2013: 93–94). Finally, there is some indication that sanctuaries and sanctuary personnel also participated in this complex system over overseers and collectors who were ultimately answerable to palatial administration (Lupack 2002).

4.5 Mycenaean Palatial Summary

Based on the extant Linear B tablets and archaeobotanical data, Mycenaean palace states were concerned with producing the same basic agricultural and non-agricultural goods that were the focus of the previous Minoan palatial regime. However, the ways in which the central bureaucracy acquired these goods were much more intrusive. At all palaces where documents have been preserved in some quantity (namely Pylos and Knossos), there is a clear indication that even if the palace did not control outright the land on which staple crops were grown, it was nevertheless invested in the management of large swaths of land either through various types of overseers and collectors, or through taxes and assessments. In addition, the tablets indicate that each palace, while having similar systems of production in place, such as the *ta-ra-si-ja*, had their own specialties and variations of management. Knossos maintained a similar ratio of grain (*120) to other products as the previous Minoan system at Hagia Triada, while focusing much of their attention on textile production and the management of sheep flocks. Pylos, however, did not have such a stark difference between the quantity of grain (*120) and other goods produced and seemed to specialize in flax and the production of linen textiles. No matter what emphasis existed, Mycenaean central bureaucracy was able to control most of the resources drawn from the kingdom as a whole, while maintaining some palatial estates. Finally, it is also clear that Mycenaean palatial states were more concerned with the direct management of added-value non-agrarian goods, such as metal objects and perfume. This concern is made evident not only through detailed administrative documentation, but also through archaeological remains of workshops located in and around palatial buildings. When palatial bureaucracy collapsed at the end of the Late Helladic IIIB period, control over these items and the mechanisms for their production dispersed, a topic to which we will now turn.

5 The Postpalatial Era

In the decades around 1200 BCE, the Mycenaean palaces underwent catastrophic change to the point where all of them suffered some sort of destruction. Explanations for why the Mycenaean palaces all seem to have undergone either total or partial collapse around the same time are many and varied (Dickinson 2010; Middleton 2010; Maran 2011). Both internal and external stimuli seem to have played a role and may have worked together to bring down the political and economic structures in place during the palatial Bronze Age. Earthquakes, droughts, and influxes of new people, even nonhostiles, are some of the more popular external causes attributed to the collapse. While some of the Mycenaean palace sites were reoccupied almost immediately (e.g. Tiryns, Mycenae, Midea, and Argos), others were mostly abandoned (e.g. Pylos). Other non-palatial sites were reoccupied or newly established and seem to have prospered for multiple generations. Some of the most prominent non-palatial sites include Aigeira in Achaia, Korakou in the Corinthia, Lefkandi on the island of Euboea, and many sites in coastal Lokris, Phocis, and Attica (Lemos 2014: 171). This era of regeneration lasting around 150 years (ca. 1200–1050) is called the Postpalatial era and is referred to as Late Helladic (LH) IIIC or Late Minoan (LM) IIIC in ceramic chronological terms.

The hierarchy and social structure of Postpalatial settlements is debated, but surely differed from the previous palatial regime. The construction of multiple large buildings within a single settlement might signal the emergence of independent *oikoi* or households, individuals from which might have made up a ruling class. However, the nature of this hierarchy is unknown predominantly because along with the collapse of the palaces came the loss of writing in Linear B. Without any written documents, we must rely solely on archaeological remains to understand the types of agricultural and non-agricultural goods produced during the Postpalatial era. Certainly, the political and socioeconomic changes resulting from the collapse of the palaces would have produced significant alterations to systems of production. In what follows, I will outline what evidence we have for the types of goods produced and their patterns of production and storage.

5.1 Agricultural Goods

Archaeobotanical remains from multiple LH IIIC sites indicate that most, if not all, of the types of agricultural produce planted or raised in the palatial era continued to be cultivated in the ensuing Postpalatial era.[75] A growing body of archaeobotanical evidence indicates that after the palaces collapsed, towns, especially those not previously highly integrated with a palace economy, continued to produce the same individual components of the palatial-period agricultural system (Foxhall 1995; Schachl 2006 [Aigeira]; Livarda & Kotzamani 2006 [Xeropolis]; Pasternak 2006 [Tiryns]). In general, and where information is available, it seems that Postpalatial socioeconomic management on both the Greek mainland and Crete supported a broad agricultural strategy that included the cultivation of different species of cereal, legumes, and fruit (Lemos 2014: 178). Of course, the biggest difficulty with having only archaeobotanical

---

[75] Sedimentary cores from lake beds and the palynological (pollen) evidence contained therein broadly corroborate these data from archaeological sites, but only those sites close to the core location (Finné et al. 2011: 3166; Kouli 2011).

evidence at hand is that it can only provide evidence for the presence of an agricultural good – not its absence or its relative quantity. Variable sampling techniques and protocols at each site make it even more difficult to draw any conclusions. However, in what follows, I outline some of the evidence for the presence, at least, of agricultural goods at Postpalatial sites.

5.1.1 Grain

Both reoccupied palatial and non-palatial sites produced evidence for the continued production of barley and wheat during the Postpalatial era. Indeed, there might have even been an increase in the quality of vegetation and crops during this time period. Grain from the LH IIIC Argolid was larger and better quality than during the previous palatial era (Deger-Jalkotzy 1998: 122). It has been suggested that the palatial collapse created a context for vast amounts of land to regenerate and renew, making crop production much less strenuous. In LH IIIC levels at Mycenae, emmer wheat and barley were found in the remains of pithoi and small tubs (Wace 1921–23: 49; Hillman 2011). In a non-palatial context, buildings on the acropolis at Aigeira contained bins full of barley (Alram-Stern 2003: 19). And at Lefkandi, storage bins and pithoi were found with remains of spelt mixed with barley (Popham and Sackett 1968: 11–13). Although these are only a few examples, the general trend in archaeobotanical record is a dominance in the presence of barley over wheat (Foxhall 1995). Whether this is a result of variability in sampling strategies and preservation or is a real reflection of agricultural trends in the LH IIIC period is hard to say.

5.1.2 Fruit

Many storage and occupation areas in Postpalatial settlement contexts contain remains of olives and grapes. Archaeobotanical remains from Nichoria and Methana suggest that virtually the same subsistence crops continued to grow into the Early Iron Age, including olives and grapes. At Korakou, a large quantity of carbonized olive stones was found fallen between the central building's earthen platform and column base (Blegen 1921: 86, n. 1). In addition, figs were found in bins in the LH IIIC levels of the site at Aigeira (Alram-Stern 2003: d 19) and in storage contexts at Lefkandi (Popham & Sackett 1968: 11–13). These are only a few examples of a general trend that suggests people living in Postpalatial Greece continued to cultivate grape vines, olive trees, and fig trees.

5.1.3 Legumes

In the Postpalatial era, legumes continue to be present in most robust archae-obotanical assemblages. This is perhaps not surprising since legumes had been present throughout the Minoan and Mycenaean palatial eras. What is perhaps more intriguing is whether the presence of legumes intensifies after the collapse of the palatial regime, which as we have seen, was much more focused on the surplus production of grains and the complete disregard for legumes (despite their use). Buildings on the acropolis at Aigeira contained bins full of beans and vetches, along with grains (Alram-Stern 2003: 19). In LH IIIC levels of Mycenae, bitter vetch was found in the remains of pithoi and small tubs also alongside grain (Wace 1921–23: 49; Hillman 2011). The presence of beans and vetches alongside more traditional grains like barley and wheat might suggest that these were all considered staple foods for the time period, and therefore outside of a hierarchy where wheat might have been considered more desirable.

5.2 Nonagricultural Goods

In her work on the Late Bronze Age and Early Iron Age Greek economy, Sarah Murray (2012, 2017) examined in detail the evidence for production of textiles, pottery, and metals at excavated settlement sites. The data indeed indicate marked changes in the location and extent of production between the Palatial and Postpalatial eras. Specifically, there was a meaningful decrease in the scale of industrial production after the palatial collapse, with large complexes like those at Poros-Katsambas and Kommos falling out of use, and replaced by localized small-scale work at individual sites (Murray 2012: 209). Ceramics, which had not been produced within major settlements in LM/LH IIIB, were made and fired on a village-by-village basis in the LM/LH IIIC period. In addition, some regions seem to have specialized in certain types of wares or shapes, such as White Ware (Murray & Lis 2023), and small, decorated stirrup jars. These fine stirrup jars, which are mainly found in large numbers in tombs, are also proxies for the liquids contained within. In this case, the most likely substance was perfumed oil. The predominance of this shape in funerary contexts suggests that a healthy perfumed oil industry also continued after the palatial collapse, at least in some locations (Pratt 2021: 175–78). Based on archaeological remains of textile tools, evidence for textile production is simi-larly distributed throughout households and villages. Both linen and wool textiles continued to be produced using similar weaving technologies and styles (Gleba 2017). In addition, after the collapse of the palaces, centralized control of the bronze industry likewise dissolved, which led to local communities having access to metal resources and their trade. The result was a sudden explosion in the use of bronze for personal adornment, along with new import distributions in the LM/LH IIIC period.

5.3 Postpalatial Systems of Production?

While there is no question that the main crops of the palatial era continued to be produced, the scale of production and where it took place or who was involved are hard to pinpoint. That some products, such as grain, wine, and olives continued to be produced in surplus can be seen through the evidence of storage facilities. Instead of being funneled into palatial storerooms, in the Postpalatial era surplus seems to have been contained in individual households or communal buildings (Lemos 2014: 177). For example, at Tiryns, Building T on top of the old Mycenaean megaron was associated with a row of twelve pithoi, interpreted as holding supplies for feasts (Maran 2001: 118, fig. 4.1). In addition, many rooms in the Lower Citadel contained storage containers and unbaked clay bins (Kilian 1988). Rooms 106/106a also contained equipment for consuming and storing wine and oil including a trefoil jug, a stirrup jar, four kraters, and many stirrup jar stoppers, one of which had a seal with a goat impressed nine times on it (Thomatos 2006: 193). At Mycenae, pithoi seem to have been found through-out the LH IIIC levels (Sherratt 1981: 78). Just like Tiryns, pithoi were also accompanied by bins made of unbaked clay. At the Granary, Wace mentions two pithoi and "the rest – and they were many – were vessels in shape like small tubs about 0.70 m high and 0.50 m in diameter, with thick walls of unbaked clay" (Wace 1921–23: 48).

Sites that had no palatial past also show evidence for increased storage capacity within or near large houses in the LH IIIC period. The substantial buildings found on the acropolis at Aigeira also have evidence for multiple large storage rooms containing bins and kilns. During Phase Ib of the LH IIIC site, the household area included a pottery kiln and storage room with two clay bins set on the floor and filled with carbonized fruit. One amphora was found lying on a clay platform. The kiln and storage room lined a courtyard in which was a large clay bin filled with ashes (Alram-Stern 2003: 19). The large Postpalatial site of Kynos, located on the coast of Lokris, has also produced evidence for large storage areas, as well as industrial activities. Most buildings contained storage areas and the discovery of kilns provides evidence that workshops were also housed in the buildings (Kramer-Hajos 2008: 39). In one house, an LH IIIC clay floor contained many pithoi in situ used as a storage facility (AD 40, pl. 59). Other pithoi with seeds and round, clay storage bins in earlier floor levels suggest the area was used as storage quarters in at least three consecutive phases, indicating that agricultural produce from the plain of Atalanti was stored centrally at Kynos (Kramer-Hajos 2008: 39). Lefkandi too had a decentralized storage strategy, with most houses having excellent storage capacities (Lemos 2014: 171). Phase 1 has at least nine circular bins of unbaked clay and other clay receptacles and large storage pithoi (Popham & Sackett 1968: 11–13). Phase 2 had more unbaked clay bins. Storage areas were incorporated in house complexes alongside other functions – usually pertaining to food preparation. In all these cases, the desire to continue producing labor-intensive surplus commodities may have been triggered by competition in the form of conspicuous consumption and control over resources, an aspect of social life that had clearly continued from the Palatial period.

5.4 Postpalatial Summary

The changes in scale and location of production outlined earlier indicate that after the palatial administration disappeared, economic scale, and structure were altered significantly at the same time that people continued to produce familiar agricultural and non-agricultural goods. While LB IIIB sites show limited material indication of the production of many everyday goods, LB IIIC sites, in contrast, show "remarkable and wide-ranging evidence of industrial activity" (Murray 2012: 207). We therefore see a shift from centralized, large-scale production to localized, smaller-scale production for both agricultural and non-agricultural goods.

6 Summary and Conclusions

6.1 Summary: Comparative Economics

Analyzing key products and modes of production from the Minoan palatial era to the Postpalatial era allows us to see a few patterns of similarity and change from one distinctive political regime to another. While people produced the same types of goods from the same types of raw materials in all three time periods, the scale and regulation of production changed. In the Minoan Neopalatial period, grain is most clearly represented by one ideogram (AB 120) in the written records but it can have over fourteen different types of ligatures or variants. Grain is by far the most prevalent agricultural product represented with over 500,000 liters listed in the extant tablets alone (which are limited to begin with and concentrated at one site). Moreover, the amount of grain listed is over twelve times greater than the second most voluminous product, figs. In contrast, grain in the Linear B tablets of the Mycenaean palatial era is listed as two obvious products (*120 and *121), and they are not modified by, presumably, descriptive or meaningful ligatures. Interestingly, at Knossos, *120 totals almost 1.5 million liters, whereas *121 totals a little over 3,300 liters (see section 4.1.1). Therefore, *120 accounts for over 99 percent of the total grain recorded at the Mycenaean palace at Knossos. This is very consistent with the percentage of AB 120 over A 303 in the previous Neopalatial period, perhaps suggesting a continuity in production strategies in relation to, specifically, types of grain. In contrast, the tablets from Pylos provide a very different picture. Here, both grains are represented almost equally, but in very different contexts from each other and in much smaller quantities than Knossos. This comparison highlights both the continuity in Crete from one political regime to another, and the differences in production strategy between one Mycenaean palatial state and another. These differences are emphasized when one takes into account the numerous records from Pylos dealing with flax, a product that does not seem to have been important at Knossos.

In the Minoan Neopalatial era, figs are the second most represented agricultural commodity in written records. Almost 80,000 liters of figs are recorded in the extant tablets and are often listed in similar contexts as grain or on totaling tablets, likely reflecting palatial collection. Unlike grain, olive oil, and wine, figs do not receive any ligatures or descriptive additions. Figs retain an important place in Mycenaean records and are often used to supplement rations of grain. Quantities vary, but can be as large as 60,000 liters for a single entry, suggesting a continued emphasis on their production.

Olives are not as frequently listed in Neopalatial texts, are often in smaller quantities, and listed with other commodities. About 18,000 liters of olives are recorded on the extant Linear A texts. As whole fruits, and similar to figs, olives only receive one ligature (as opposed to the fourteen recorded for grain and olive oil). This might suggest that the ligatures have more to do with processing agricultural goods rather than the economic context, production mode, origin, or destination. Interestingly, olives are recorded in much larger relative quantities in the Mycenaean documents. At Knossos a total of almost 80,000 liters of olives is recorded. However, a similar ratio of grain to figs to olives is maintained from the Neopalatial era to the Mycenaean palatial era on Crete.

Olive oil is listed in extremely small amounts and very frequently in Neopalatial texts (ninety-six times at Hagia Triada but only 13,881.6 liters compared to, e.g. olives listed only fourteen times and amounting to over 16,000 liters). It also receives many ligatures (over fourteen on the extant tablets), suggesting variations in quality, type of oil, or scents. Mycenaean olive oil entries at Knossos are larger than the previous era, which is consistent with other goods. Like the Neopalatial era, it is often recorded in smaller amounts and is found in almost every type of record, including perfume manufacture, something that the Minoans did not seem to record with written texts, at least.

In the Neopalatial era, wine is listed at most sites where Linear A has been found, and at Hagia Triada, it is recorded in similar quantities to olives and oil, with almost 14,000 liters total. However, because it is listed at many other sites, including rural villas, the total amount of wine listed in all the tablets is about 27,500 liters. Unlike olive oil, wine is generally listed in much larger quantities per entry. Wine frequently appears with other commodities, but it also has its own totaling tablets, suggesting palatial concern with collecting larger quantities of this specific product. Interestingly, wine is not recorded in large quantities in Mycenaean records. Only about 16,000 liters were listed at both Knossos and Pylos, each. However, the 16,000 liters at Pylos make up a greater percentage of the total agricultural goods recorded than at Knossos.

Livestock is not a major factor in Neopalatial records. Very few animals are recorded, and even sheep only have 100 as their largest entry. Of course, this could be due to the limited nature of the extant tablets. However, since all of the other major domestic products discussed earlier are listed, it is strange that a product so important to the following Mycenaean palatial era would be missing entirely. Indeed, the Mycenaean records at Knossos imply oversight of over 100,000 sheep of various kinds and ages under the care of as many as 590 shepherds.[76] About one-third of the total tablets found at this palace concerned sheep and similar preoccupation has been suggested for Pylos where 154 individuals are listed as responsible for flocks.

People in both the Minoan and Mycenaean palatial eras cultivated foodstuffs outside of the products listed in the written documents. Palaeobotanical evidence clearly supports the cultivation of legumes and vetches of various kinds. Moreover, these goods are often found alongside things like barley and wheat in storerooms, especially outside of palatial contexts. This proximity suggests that Aegean cultures in general practiced a mixed farming strategy that used all available types of complex carbohydrates for both animal and human consumption. Palatial concern with specific grains suggests a value system whereby AB 120 and *120/*121 were more conducive to palatial interests. In this case, these specific grains had a use and an exchange value, making them true commodities in the Marxist sense. The commodities represented by *120/*121 were used for payments, rations, and gifts–exchanges that go beyond simple redistributive subsistence. It is unclear exactly how Neopalatial authorities used the vast amounts of grain recorded in the Linear A tablets, but similar exchanges are likely.

---

[76] On the shepherds at Knossos, their names, and their locations, see Olivier 1988. Some of these entries are illegible, are debated, and are listed more than once (whether it is the same person or two shepherds with the same name is debated).

The same types of derivative and non-agricultural goods were produced in the Minoan and Mycenaean palatial eras. Pottery, textiles, perfumed oil, and finished products using imported metals were consistently produced. However, extant textual data indicates that the Minoan palatial authorities were not interested in regulating the production of the raw materials, in the case of wool and olive oil, or in regulating the production of finished products. There is more concern with the collection of those products. In contrast, Mycenaean texts from both Knossos and Pylos indicate a much more hands-on approach to regulating both the raw materials and the finished products. Although palatial authorities acquired finished products through different modes of production, the end result was the same. This does not mean that Mycenaean palaces controlled directly the flocks, fields, and orchards, but rather, that they took an interest in overseeing and keeping track of the products from those places and the people who did have control over them. This regulation was once again loosened in the Postpalatial era when production of both agricultural and non-agricultural goods was reduced in scale and shifted to local or even household manufacturing. The resiliency of Aegean Bronze Age production is most evident in the consistency of products, allowing for some variation in emphasis, across centuries and despite changing political regimes.

6.2 Future Research and New Analyses

This overview and analysis of Mycenaean domestic production highlights a few avenues for future research and a few lacunae, the filling of which would improve our understanding tremendously. Perhaps the most irritating gap is the inability to securely identify certain ideograms with a particular product. The debate surrounding whether AB 120/*120 is wheat or barley is the most obvious. The only way to really end this debate would be to associate the sign with archaeobotanical remains. It is therefore imperative that careful records are kept for the findspots of plant remains. As mentioned at the outset, archaeobotanical remains are invaluable pieces of information about past foodways and economies. However, in previous archaeological campaigns they have been variably recorded or sampled. More and better ways of sampling plant remains have made their results much more compelling and useful for answering a number of questions about past people and their diets. Standardized ways of sampling will help to even out archaeobotanical data from different sites so that comparisons are more easily drawn.

In addition, a number of new scientific methods have developed over the past few years that indicate a bright future for complex analyses of micro-remains such as dental calculus and organic residues, as well as various isotopic analyses.

Organic residue analysis has been used for a few decades, but the methods of extraction and the resolution of results continue to improve. Previous residue analyses have been useful for not only confirming some suspicions about what certain containers held, but also challenging our biased views about others. Now that residue analysis is a more standard aspect of archaeological research, projects are better equipped to plan ahead and refrain from cleaning or contaminating certain vessels that seem promising for testing. Once vessels are cleaned vigorously, they are much more difficult to sample successfully. As with palaeobotanical research, a more progressive and anticipatory approach is best when adopting a program of residue analysis. Residues are not only left in ceramic vessels, but in unlikely places like dental calculus. As one of the newer avenues of research, dental calculus analysis holds great potential for helping to answer questions about diet, health, and even the environment. The latter is perhaps exemplified by the discovery of lignite coal particles in the calculus of Mycenean people, discussed earlier (Buckley et al. 2021).

Finally, isotopic approaches are a recent and promising new direction for palaeobotanical and zooarchaeological questions. Using ancient ruminant tooth enamel, researchers have been able to employ multi-isotope analysis to explore the life histories of sheep and goats and the various ways in which people controlled or directed their consumption of food. Using this method, ancient herding regimes, fodder supplementation, and environmental exploitation for animal husbandry can be more clearly understood. In their work on the Bronze Age herds of sheep and goats at Knossos, Isaakidou et al. (2019) used stable carbon, oxygen, and strontium isotope ratios in dental enamel bioapatite of ancient sheep and goats to see differences in diet over time. What they found was that the sheep and goats sampled, although few in number, broadly matched the strategies implied by the Linear B records, including movement of sheep according to seasonal availability of food, and supplemental fodder for goats. Subsequently, Isaakidou et al. (2022) used similar isotopic techniques on charred crop grains and faunal bone collagen to elucidate growing conditions and types of fodder consumed, respectively, from a long-term perspective at Knossos. Their work included samples from Final Neolithic to Final Palatial levels of Knossos and determined that cultivation and animal husbandry techniques changes throughout these time periods with some crops receiving more water than others at certain times (e.g. Final Palatial Knossos grew pulses and barley in different plots of land and in rotation with emmer wheat, which received supplemental irrigation; Isaakidou et al. 2022: 166). In addition, their analyses of faunal remains determined that sheep grazing techniques reflected in the isotopic changes represent an increasing scale of herding, and goats were herded separately from sheep (Isaakidou et al. 2022: 174). Their work highlights the ways in which detailed scientific analyses can help answer big questions about long-term agricultural change when given access to sufficient resources and sample sizes. Future research using isotopic analyses will likely involve even larger sample sizes and comparative approaches with data from different contemporary sites. The new techniques discussed here highlight the ever-evolving nature of archaeological discovery and the possibilities for future avenues of research just in their infancy.

References

Alberti, M. E., Müller Celka, S., & Pomadère, M. (2019). The management of agricultural resources in the Minoan town of Malia (Crete) from the Middle Bronze Age to the Early Late Bronze Age. In D. Garcia, R. Orgeolet, M. Pomadère, & J. Zurbach, eds., *Country in the City: Agricultural Functions of Protohistoric Urban Settlements (Aegean and Western Mediterranean)*. Oxford: Archaeopress, pp. 51–71.

Alram-Stern, E. (2003). Aigeira-akropolis: The stratigraphy. In S. Deger-Jalkotzy, & M. Zavadil, eds., *Late Helladic IIIC Chronology and Synchronisms: Proceedings of the International Workshop Held at the Austrian Academy of Sciences at Vienna, May 7th and 8th, 2001, Vienna*. Wien: Verlag der Österreichischen Akademie der Wissenschaften, Österreichische Akademie der Wissenschaften philosophisch-historische Klasse Denkscriften, pp. 15–21.

Apostolaki, E. (2014). *Η δυναμική του οικιακού χώρου: Παραδείγματα νοικοκυριών από τη νεοανακτορική κοινωνία της Κρήτης*. Unpublished PhD Thesis University of Athens. For an online version see http://phdtheses.ekt.gr/eadd/handle/10442/34656.

Aravantinos, V., & Vasilogamvrou, A. (2012). The first Linear B documents from Ayios Vasileios (Laconia). In P. Carlier, C. de Lamberterie, M. Egetmeyer, et al., eds., *Études mycéniennes 2010: actes du XIIIe Colloque international sur les textes égéens: Sèvres, Paris, Nanterre, 20–23 septembre 2010*. Pisa: F. Serra, pp. 41–54.

Aura Jorro, F. (1993). *Diccionario Micénico, Vol. II*. Madrid: Consejo Superior de Investigaciones Cientificas.

Bendall, L. M. (2001). The economics of Potnia in the Linear B documents: Palatial support for Mycenaean religion. In R. Laffineur, & R. Hägg, eds., *Potnia: Deities and Religion in the Aegean Bronze Age [Aegaeum 22]*. Liège: Université de Liège, pp. 445–52.

Bendall, L. M. (2007a). *Economics of Religion in the Mycenaean World: Resources Dedicated to Religion in the Mycenaean Palace Economy*. Oxford: School of Archaeology.

Bendall, L. M. (2007b). How much makes a feast? Amounts of banqueting foodstuffs in the Linear B records of Pylos. In A. Sacconi, M. Del Freo, L. Godart, & M. Negri, eds., *Colloquium Romanum: Atti del XII Colloquio Internazionale di Micenologia*. Pisa: F. Serra, pp. 77–101.

Bendall, L. M. (2014). Gifts to the goddesses: Pylian perfumed olive oil abroad? In W. Shelmerdine, D. Nakassis, J. Gulizio, & S. A. James, eds., *KE-RA-ME-*

JA: Studies Presented to Cynthia Shelmerdine. INSTAP Prehistory Mono graphs 46. Philadelphia, PA: INSTAP Academic Press, pp. 141–62.

Bennet, J. (1985). The structure of the Linear B administration at Knossos. *AJA* **89**, 231–49.

Bennet, J. (1992). "Collectors" or "Owners"? An examination of their possible functions within the palatial economy of LM III Crete. In J.-P. Olivier, ed., *Mykenaïka. Actes Du IXe Colloque International Sur Les Textes Mycéniens et Égéens Organisé Par Le Centre de l'Antiquité Grecque et Romaine de La Fondation Hellénique Des Recherches Scientifiques et l'École Fran\ccaise d'Athènes (Athènes, 2–6 Octobre 1990)*. Athens: École française d'Athènes, pp. 65–101.

Bennett, E. (2002). What must we know about Minoan and Mycenaean wine? In A. K. Mylopotamitaki, ed., *Oinos Palaios Idypotos: To Kritiko Krasi apo ta Proïstorika os ta Neotera Chronia. Kounavoi: Dimos 'N. Kazantzakis', 24–26 Apriliou 1998*. Irakleio: Ypourgeio Politismou Archaiologiko Institouto Kritis, Praktika tou Diethnous Epistimonikou Symposiou, pp. 77–85.

Bennet, J. (2008). Palace ™ : Speculations on palatial production in Mycenaean Greece with (some) reference to glass. In C. M. Jackson, & E. C. Wager, eds., *Vitreous Materials in the Late Bronze Age Aegean (Sheffield Studies in Aegean Archaeology 9)*. Oxford: Oxbow Books. pp. 151–72.

Bennet, J., & Halstead, P. (2014). O-no! Writing and righting redistribution. In D. Nakassis, J. Gulizio, & S. A. James, eds., *KE-RA-ME-JA: Studies Presented to Cynthia W. Shelmerdine*. Philadelphia, PA: INSTAP Academic Press, pp. 271–82.

Bennett Jr., E. L. (1985). The first Mycenaean inscribed tablets ever found on the Greek Mainland. In N. C. Wilkie, & W. D. E. Coulson, eds., *Contributions to Aegean Archaeology: Studies in Honor of William A. McDonald*. Publications in Ancient Studies 1. Minneapolis: Center for Ancient Studies, University of Minnesota, pp. 37–48.

Blegen, C. W. (1921). *Korakou: A Prehistoric Settlement Near Corinth*. Boston, MA: American School of Classical Studies at Athens.

Blegen, C. W., & Rawson, M. (1966). *The Palace of Nestor at Pylos in Western Messenia, Vol. 1: The Buildings and Their Context*. Princeton, NJ: Princeton University Press.

Blitzer, H. (1995). Minoan implements and industries. In J. W. Shaw, & M. C. Shaw, eds., *Kommos I, Part I*. Princeton, NJ: Princeton University Press, pp. 403–535.

Boulotis, C. (1998). Les nouveaux documents en linéaire A d'Akrotiri (Théra): remarques préliminaires. In F. Rougemont, & J.-P. Olivier, eds., *Recherches récentes en épigraphie créto-mycénienne.* BCH 122. Paris: École Française d'Athènes, pp. 407–11.

Brogan, T., & Koh, A. (2008). Feasting at Mochlos? New evidence for wine pro-duction, storage and consumption from a Bronze Age harbor town on Crete. In L. Hitchcock, R. Laffineur, & J. Crowley, eds., *Dais: The Aegean Feast* (Aegaeum 29). Liège: Université de Liège, Histoire de l'art et archéologie de la Grèce antique, pp. 125–31.

Buckley, S., R. C. Power, M. Andreadaki-Vlazaki, et al. (2021). Archaeometric evidence for the earliest exploitation of lignite from the Bronze Age eastern Mediterranean. *Nature: Scientific Reports* **11**, 24185.

Christakis, K. S. (2008). *The Politics of Storage: Storage and Sociopolitical Complexity in Neopalatial Crete* (Prehistory Monographs 25). Philadelphia, PA: INSTAP Academic Press.

Christakis, K. S. (2019). The neglected "fields" of proto-urban living: A view from Bronze Age Crete. In D. Garcia, R. Orgeolet, M. Pomadère, & J. Zurbach, eds., *Country in the City: Agricultural Functions of Protohistoric Urban Settlements (Aegean and Western Mediterranean)*. Oxford: Archaeopress, pp. 41–50.

Davis, B. (2013). Syntax in Linear A: The word-order of the "Libation Formula." *Kadmos* **52(1)**, 35–52.

De Fidio, P. (2024a). The absolute values for the symbols for weight. In J. Killen, ed., *The New Documents in Mycenaean Greek*. Cambridge: Cambridge University Press, pp. 137–68.

De Fidio, P. (2024b). The absolute values of the symbols for volume. In J. Killen, ed., *The New Documents in Mycenaean Greek*. Cambridge: Cambridge University Press, pp. 169–204.

Decorte, R. P.-J. E. (2017). Cretan Hieroglyphic and the nature of script. In P. M. Steele, ed., *Understanding Relations between Scripts: The Aegean Writing Systems*. Oxford: Oxford University Press, pp. 33–56.

Decorte, R. P.-J. E. (2018). The origins of Bronze Age Aegean writing: Linear A, Cretan Hieroglyphic and a new proposed pathway of script formation. In S. Ferrara, & M. Valério, eds., *Paths into Script Formation in the Ancient Mediterranean, Studi Micenei ed Egeo-Anatolici* (n.s., supplement 1). Rome: Edizioni Quasar, pp. 13–49.

Deger-Jalkotzy, S. (1998). Die mykenische Peripherie und die Entwicklung politischer Organisationformen von der mykenischen bis zur archaischen Ära. In N. Dimoudis, & A. Kyriatsoulis, eds., *Die Geschichte der hellenischen Sprache und Schrift vom 2. zum 1. Jahrtausend v. Chr.: Bruch oder Kontinuität?* Altenburg: DZA Verl. für Kultur und Wissenschaft, pp. 331–43.

Del Freo, M. (2024). The Linear B documents. In J. Killen, ed., *The New Documents in Mycenaean Greek*. Cambridge: Cambridge University Press, pp. 205–31.

Del Freo, M., Nosch, M.-L., & Rougemont, F. (2010). The terminology of textiles in the Linear B tablets, including some considerations on Linear A logograms and abbreviations. In C. Michel, & M.-L. Nosch, eds., *Textile Terminologies in the Ancient Near East and Mediterranean from the Third to the First Millennium BC*. Oxford: Oxbow Books, pp. 338–73.

Dickinson, O. (2006). *The Aegean from Bronze Age to Iron Age: Continuity and Change between the Twelfth and Eighth Centuries BC*. New York: Routledge.

Driessen, J. (2008). Chronology of the Linear B texts. In Y. Duhoux, & A. Morpurgo Davies, eds., *A Companion to Linear B: Mycenaean Greek Texts and Their World, vol. I*. Leuven: Peeters, pp. 68–79.

Driessen, J. (2018). Beyond the collective . . . The Minoan palace in action. In I. Papadatos, & M. Relaki, eds., *From the Foundations to the Legacy of Minoan Archaeology: Sheffield Studies in Honor of Keith Branigan*. Oxford: Oxbow Books, pp. 291–313.

Driessen, J., & Macdonald, C. F. (1997). *The Troubled Island: Minoan Crete before and after the Santorini Eruption* (Aegaeum 17). Austin: The University of Texas at Austiin Press.

Driessen, J., & Mouthuy, O. (2022). The LM II-IIIA2 Kingdom of Knossos as reflected by its Linear B archives. *SMEA NS* **2**, 71–84.

Duhoux, Y. (2008). Mycenaean anthology. In Y. Duhoux, & A. Morpurgo Davies, eds., *A Companion to Linear B: Mycenaean Greek Texts and Their World: Volume 1* (Bibliothèque des cahiers de l'Institut de Linguistique de Louvain 120). Louvain-la-Neuve: Peeters Press, pp. 243–393.

Fappas, I. (2008). The use of perfumed oils during feasting activities: A comparison of Mycenaean and Near Eastern written sources. In R. Laffineur, L. Hitchcock, & J. Crowley, eds., *DAIS, the Aegean Feast: Proceedings of the 12th International Aegean Conference Organised by the University of Melbourne and the University of Liège, Hosted by the Centre for Classics and Archaeology, Melbourne, 25–29 March 2008* (Aegaeum 29). Liege: Université de Liège, pp. 367–75.

Ferrara, S., Montecchi, B., & Valério, M. (2022). The relationship between Cretan Hieroglyphic and Linear A: A palaeographic and structural approach. *Pasiphae* **16**, 81–109.

Finné, M., Holmgren, K., Sundqvist, H. S., Weiberg, E., & Lindblom, M. (2011). Climate in the eastern Mediterranean, and adjacent regions, during the past 6000 years – a review. *Journal of Archaeological Science* **38**, 3153–73.

Firth, R. J. (1997). The find-places of the tablets from the Palace of Knossos. *Minos* **31–2**, 7–122.

Firth, R. J., & Melena, J. L. (2016). Re-visiting the scribes of the Room of the Chariot Tablets at Knossos. *Minos* **39**, 319–52.

Fischer, J. (2017). *Ernährung im mykenischen Griechenland*. Krakow: Ridero IT.

Flood, J., & Soles, J. (2014). Water management in Neopalatial Crete and the development of the Mediterranean dry-season. In G. Touchais, R. Laffineur, & F. Rougemont, eds., *Physis*. Leuven: Peeters, pp. 79–84.

Follieri, M. (1979–1980). Proviste alimentari vegetali da una casa minoica ad Haghia Triada (Creta). *AnnScAt* **42–43**, 165–72.

Foster, E. D. (1977). An administrative department at Knossos concerned with perfumery and offerings. *Minos* **16**, 19–51.

Foster, E. D. (1981). The flax impost at Pylos and Mycenaean landholdings. *Minos* **17**, 67–121.

Foxhall, L. (1995). Bronze to iron: Agricultural systems and political structures in Late Bronze Age and Early Iron Age Greece. *Annual of the British School at Athens* **90**, 239–50.

García-Granero, J. J., E. Hatzaki, E. Tsafou, et al. (2021). From storage to disposal: A holistic microbotanical approach to domestic plant preparation and consumption activities in Late Minoan Gypsades, Crete. *Journal of Archaeological Method and Theory* **28(1)**, 307–31.

Gleba, M. (2017). Tracing textile cultures of Italy and Greece in the early first millennium BC. *Antiquity* **91(359)**, 1205–22.

Godart, L. (1968). Les quantites d'huile de la serie Fh de Cnossos. In *Atti e Memorie del 1 Congresso internazionale di Micenologia*. Rome: Edizioni dell'Ateneo, pp. 598–610.

Godart, L. (1977). Les resources des palais mycéniens de Cnossos et Pylos. *ÉtCl* **45**, 31–42.

Godart, L. (1999). Les sacrifices d'animaux dans les textes myceniens. In S. Deger-Jalkotzy, S. Hiller, & O. Panagl, eds., *Floreant Studia Mycenaea. Akten des X. Internationalen Mykenologischen Colloquiums, Salzburg (DenkschrWien 274)*. Vienna: Österreichische Akademie der Wissenschaften, pp. 249–56.

Guthrie, W. K. C. (1959). Early Greek religion in the light of the decipherment of Linear B. *BICS* **6**, 35–46.

Halbherr, F., Stefani, E., & Banti, L. (1980). *Haghia Triada nel Periodo Tardo Palaziale*, AnnScAtene 55.

Haggis, D. (2005). *Kavousi I: The Archaeological Survey of the Kavousi Region*. Princeton: INSTAP Academic Press.

Hallager, E. (1996). *The Minoan Roundel and Other Sealed Documents in the Neopalatial Linear A Administration* I-II (*Aegaeum* 14). Austin: The University of Texas at Austin.

Hallager, E. (2000). The hanging nodules and their inscriptions. In M. Perna, ed., *Administrative Documents in the Aegean and Their Near Eastern Counterparts*. Turin: Paravia Scriptorium, pp. 251–60.

Halstead, P. (1995). Plough and power: The economic and social significance of cultivation with the ox-drawn ard in the Mediterranean. *Bulletin on Sumerian Agriculture* **8**, 11–22.

Halstead, P. (1998–1999). Texts, bones and herders: Approaches to animal husbandry in Late Bronze Age Greece. *Minos* **33–4**, 149–89.

Halstead, P. (1999). Surplus and share-croppers: The grain production strategies of Mycenaean palaces. In P. Betancourt, V. Karageorghis, R. Laffineur, & W.-D. Niemeier, eds., *Meletemata: Studies Presented to Malcolm H: Wiener as He Enters His 65th Year* (Aegaeum 20). Liège: Université de Liège, pp. 319–26.

Halstead, P. (2001). Mycenaean wheat, flax, and sheep: Palatial intervention in farming and its implications for rural society. In S. Voutsaki, & J. Killen, eds., *Economy and Politics in the Mycenaean Palace States: Proceedings of a Conference Held on 1–3 July 1999 in the Faculty of Classics, Cambridge* (Cambridge Philological Society Suppl. 27). Cambridge: Cambridge University Press, pp. 38–50.

Halstead, P. (2003). Texts and bones: Contrasting Linear B and archaeozoological evidence for animal exploitation in Mycenaean southern Greece. In E. Kotjabopoulou, Y. Hamilakis, P. Halstead, C. Gamble, & P. Elefanti, eds., *Zooarchaeology in Greece: Recent Advances* (BSA Studies 9). Athens: British School at Athens, pp. 257–61.

Halstead, P. (2007). Toward a model of Mycenaean Palatial mobilization. In M. L. Galaty & W. A. Parkinson, eds., *Rethinking Mycenaean Palaces II: Revised and Expanded Second Edition*. Los Angeles: The Cotsen Institute of Archaeology, pp. 66–77

Halstead, P., & Isaakidou, V. (2004). Faunal evidence for feasting: Burnt offerings from the Palace of Nestor at Pylos. In P. Halstead, & J. C. Barrett, eds., *Food, Cuisine and Society in Prehistoric Greece*. Sheffield Studies in Aegean Archaeology. Oxford: Oxbow Books, pp. 136–54.

Halstead, P., & Isaakidou, V. (2017). Sheep, sacrifices, and symbols: Animals in later Bronze Age Greece. In U. Albarella, M. Rizzetto, H. Russ, K. Vickers, & S. Viner-Daniels, eds., *The Oxford Handbook of Zooarchaeology*. Oxford: Oxford University Press, pp. 113–26.

Halstead, P., Bogaard, A., & Jones, G. (2022). Staple grains in the later Bronze Age of the (southern) Aegean: Archaeobotanical, textual and ethnographic insights. In Valamoti, A. Dimoula, & M. Ntinou, eds., *Cooking with Plants*. Leiden: Sidestone Press, pp. 93–104.

Henkel, C. & E. Margaritis (2024). Revisiting the archaeobotany of Prehistoric Crete. *American Journal of Archaeology* **128(4)**, pp. 455–91

Hiller, S. (1983). Fruchtbaumkulturen auf Kreta und in Pylos. In A. Heubeck, & G. Neumann, eds., *Res Mycenaeae. Akten des VII. Mykenologischen Colloquiums in Nürnberg vom 6.-10. April 1981*. Göttingen: Vandenhoeck & Ruprecht, pp. 171–201.

Hiller, S., & Panagl, O. (1976). *Die frühgriechischen Texte aus mykenischer Zeit*. Darmstadt: Wiss. Buchges.

Hillman, G. (2011). The grain from the granary. In E. B. French, ed., *Well Built Mycenae: Fascicule 16/17: The Post-Palatial Levels*. Oxford: Oxbow Books, pp. 748–76.

Hodder, I. (2012). *Entangled: An Archaeology of the Relationships between Humans and Things*. Malden, MA: Wiley-Blackwell.

Hruby, J. (2010). Mycenaean pottery from Pylos: An indigenous typology. *American Journal of Archaeology* **114(2)**, 195–216.

Hruby, J. (2011). *Ke-ra-me-u* or *Ke-ra-me-ja*? Evidence for sex, age and division of labour among Mycenaean ceramicists. In A. Brysbaert, ed., *Tracing Prehistoric Social Networks through Technology: A Diachronic Perspective on the Aegean*. Routledge Studies in Archaeology 3. New York: Routledge, pp. 89–105.

Hruby, J. (2013). The Palace of Nestor, craft production, and mechanisms for the transfer of goods. *American Journal of Archaeology* **117(3)**, pp. 423–27.

Isaakidou, V., Halstead, P., Davis, J. L., & Stocker, S. R. (2002). Burnt animal sacrifice at the Mycenaean "Palace of Nestor," Pylos. *Antiquity* **76(291)**, 86–92.

Isaakidou, V., A. Styring, P. Halstead, et al. (2019). From texts to teeth: A multi-isotope study of sheep and goat herding practices in the Late Bronze Age ("Mycenaean") polity of Knossos, Crete. *JAS: Reports* **23**, 36–56.

Isaakidou, V., P. Halstead, E. Stroud, et al. (2022). Changing land use and political economy at Neolithic and Bronze Age Knossos, Crete: Stable carbon ($\delta13C$) and nitrogen ($\delta15N$) isotope analysis of charred crop grains and faunal bone collagen. *Proceedings of the Prehistoric Society* **88**, 155–91.

Jasink, A. M. (2009). *Cretan Hieroglyphic Seals: A New Classification of Symbols and Ornamental/Filling Motifs, Biblioteca di Pasiphae* 13, Pisa-Rome: Rome: F. Serra.

Jung, R. (2021). Uneven and combined: Product exchange in the Mediterranean (3rd to 2nd Millennium BCE). In S. Gimatzidis, & R. Jung, eds., *The Critique of Archaeological Economy*, Frontiers in Economic History. New York: Springer, pp. 139–62.

Keßler, T. P. (2015). A royal gift? Bulk grain storage in Protopalatial and Neopalatial Crete. *SMEA NS* **1**, 1137–70.

Kilian, K. (1988). Mycenaeans up to date: Trends and changes in recent research. In E. B. French, & K. A. Wardle, eds., *Problems in Greek Prehistory: Papers Presented at the Centenary Conference of the British School of Archaeology at Athens, Manchester, April 1986*. Bristol: Bristol Classical Press, pp. 115–52.

Killen, J. T. (1964). The wool industry of Crete in the Late Bronze Age. *Annual of the British School at Athens* **59**, 1–15.

Killen, J. T. (1984). The textile industries at Pylos and Knossos. In T. G. Palaima, & C. W. Shelmerdine, eds., *Pylos Comes Alive: Industry and Administration in a Mycenaean Palace*. New York: Fordham University, pp. 49–63.

Killen, J. T. (1992–1993). The Oxen's names on the Knossos Ch tablets. *Minos* **27–28** [1995], 101–7.

Killen, J. T. (1993). Records of sheep and goats at Mycenaean Knossos and Pylos. In J. N. Postgate, & M. A. Powell, ed., *Domestic Animals of Mesopotamia, Part I, Bulletin of Sumerian Agriculture* **7**, 209–18.

Killen, J. T. (1998). The rôle of the state in wheat and olive production in Mycenaean Crete. *Aevum* **72**, 19–23.

Killen, J. T. (1999). Some observations on the new Thebes tablets. *BICS* **43**, 217–19.

Killen, J. T. (2000). Acquisition and distribution: *ta-ra-si-ja* in the Mycenaean textile industry. In C. Gillis, C. Risberg, & B. Sjöberg, eds., *Trade and Production in Premonetary Greece: Acquisition and Distribution of Raw Materials and Finished Products: Proceedings of the 6th International Workshop, Athens 1996*. Jonsered: Paul Aströms Förlag, pp. 42–62.

Killen, J. T. (2001). Some thoughts on *ta-ra-si-ja*. In S. Voutsaki, & J. Killen, eds., *Economy and Politics in the Mycenaean Palace States: Proceedings of a Conference held on 1–3 July 1999 in the Faculty of Classics, Cambridge*. Cambridge: Cambridge University Press, pp. 161–80.

Killen, J. T. (2004). Wheat, barley, flour, olives and figs on Linear B tablets. In P. Halstead, & J. C. Barrett, eds., *Food, Cuisine and Society in Prehistoric Greece*. Oxford: Oxbow Books, pp. 155–73.

Killen, J. T. (2008). The commodities on the Pylos Ma tablets. In A. Sacconi, M. Del Freo, L. Godart, & M. Negri, eds., *Colloquium Romanum: Atti del XII Colloquio internazionale di micenologia, Roma, 20–25 febbraio 2006 II* (Pasiphae 2). Pisa: Fabrizio Serra Editore, pp. 431–47.

Killen, J. T. (2015). Pylos Tablet Va 482. In M. Del Freo, ed., *Economy and Administration in Mycenaean Greece: Collected Papers on Linear B*. Roma: CNR – Istituto di Studi sul Mediterraneo Antico, pp. 835–50.

Killen, J. T. (2022). Figs and fig-trees at Knossos. In C. V. García, J. M. Dosuna, & T. G. Palaima, eds., *TA-U-RO-QO-RO: Studies in Mycenaean Texts, Language and Culture in Honor of José Luis Melena Jiménez*. Washington, DC: Center for Hellenic Studies, pp. 77–84.

Killen, J. ed. (2024) *The New Documents in Mycenaean Greek*. Cambridge: Cambridge University Press.

Kouli, K. (2011). Vegetation development and human activities in Attiki (SE Greece) during the last 5,000 years. *Vegetation History and Archaeobotany* **21**, 267–78.

Kramer-Hajos, M. (2008). *Beyond the Palace: Mycenaean East Lokris*. BAR International Series 1781. Oxford: Archaeopress.

Kroll, H. (1984). Zum Ackerbau gegen Ende der mykenischen Epoche in der Argolis. *Archäologischer Anzeiger* **1984**, 211–22.

Kroll, H. (2000). Agriculture and arboriculture in mainland Greece at the beginning of the first millennium BC. *Pallas* **52**, 61–68.

Lang, M. L. (1964). Pylos pots and the Mycenaean units of capacity. *American Journal of Archaeology* **68**, 95–105.

Lemos, I. (2014). Communities in transformation: An archaeological survey from the 12th to the 9th century BC. *Pharos* **20(1)**, 161–92.

Levi, D., & Laviosa, C. (1979–80). Il forno minoico da vasaio di Haghia Triada. *AnnScAt* **41–42**, 7–47.

Livarda, A., & Kotzamani, G. (2006). Plant lore in "Dark Age" Greece: Archaeobotanical evidence from Lefkandi, Euboea, literal sources and traditional knowledge combined. In Z. F. Ertug, ed., *Proceedings of the IVth International Congress of Ethnobotany (ICEB 2005)*. İstanbul: Efe Yayinlari, pp. 435–37.

Livarda, A., & Kotzamani, G. (2013). The archaeobotany of Neolithic and Bronze Age Crete: Synthesis and prospects. *The Annual of the British School at Athens* **108**, 1–29.

Lupack, S. (2002). *The Role of the Religious Sector in the Economy of Late Bronze Age Mycenaean Greece*. Unpublished PhD Dissertation. The University of Texas at Austin.

Lupack, S. (2007). Palaces, sanctuaries, and workshops: The role of the religious sector in Mycenaean economics. In M. L. Galaty, & W. A. Parkinson, eds., *Rethinking Mycenaean Palaces II (UCLAMon 60)*. Los Angeles, CA: Cotsen Institute Press, pp. 54–63.

Maran, J. (2001). Political and religious aspects of architectural change on the Upper Citadel of Tiryns: The case of Building T. In R. Laffineur, & R. Hägg, eds., *Potnia: Deities and Religion in the Aegean Bronze Age* (Aegaeum 22). Liège: Université de Liège, pp. 113–22.

Maran, J. (2011). Contested pasts – The society of the 12th c. B.C.E. Argolid and the memory of the Mycenaean palatial period. In W. Gauß, M. Lindblom, R. A. K. Smith, & J. C. Wright, eds., *Our Cups Are Full: Pottery and Society in the Aegean Bronze Age: Papers Presented to Jeremy B. Rutter on the Occasion of His 65th Birthday*. Oxford: Archaeopress, pp. 169–78.

Margaritis, E., Demakopoulou, K., & Schallin, A.-L. (2014). The archaeobotanical samples from Midea: Agricultural choices in the Mycenaean Argolid. In G. Touchais, R. Laffineur, & F. Rougemont, eds., *PHYSIS. L'environment naturel et al relation homme-milieu dans le monde Égéen protohistorique: Actes de la 14 Rencontre égéen international, Paris, Institut National d'Histoire de l'Art (INHA), 11–14 décembre 2012*. Leuven: Peeters, pp. 271–79.

Mattoïan, V. (2004). Influence des productions mycéniennes à Ougarit (Syrie): l'exemple des vases à étrier "en faïence. In J. Balensi, J.-Y. Monchambert, & S. Müller Celka, eds., *La céramique mycénienne de l'Égée au Levant: Hommage à Vronwy Hankey* (Travaux de la maison de l'Orient et de la Méditerranée 41). Lyon: Maison de l'Orient et de la Méditerranée, pp. 105–24.

Melena, J. L. (1983). Olive oil and other sorts of oil in the Mycenaean tablets. *Minos* **28**, 89–123.

Middleton, G. (2010). *The Collapse of Palatial Society in LBA Greece and the Postpalatial Period*. BAR 2110. Oxford: Archaeopress.

Militello, P., O. Palio, & M. Figuera. (2020). Houses, central buildings and embedded production. In M. Relaki & J. Driessen, eds., *Oikos: Archaeological Approaches to "House Societies" in the Bronze Age Aegean*. Aegis 19. Louvain: Presses Universitaires de Louvain, pp. 121–40.

Montecchi, B. (2012). Linear A banqueting lists? *Kadmos* **51**, 1–26.

Montecchi, B. (2019). *Contare a Haghia Triada: Le tavolette in lineare A, I documenti sigillati e il Sistema economica-amministrativo nel TM IB*. Incunabulae Graeca CVII. Rome: CNR Edizioni.

Morgan, C. (2015). The work of the British School at Athens 2014–15. *Archaeological Reports* **61**, 34–48.

Morris, S. P. (1992). *Daidalos and the Origins of Greek Art*. Princeton, NJ: Princeton University Press.

Morris, S. P. (2001). Potnia Aswiya: Anatolian contributions to Greek religion. In R. Laffineur, & R. Hägg, eds., *Potnia: Deities and Religion in the Aegean Bronze Age*. Austin: University of Texas at Austin, pp. 423–34.

Murphy, J. M. A. (2012). The scent of status: Prestige and perfume at the Bronze Age palace at Pylos, Greece. In J. Day, ed., *Making Senses of the Past: Toward a Sensory Archaeology*. Center for Archaological Investigations, Occasional Paper No. 40. Carbondale: Southern Illinois University, pp. 243–65.

Murray, C. M. (1979). *Mycenaean Religion: The Evidence of the Linear B Tablets* (unpublished PhD dissertation). University of Cambridge, Girton College.

Murray, S. C. (2012). *Trade, Imports, and Society in Early Greece: 1300–900 B.C.E.* Ph.D. dissertation, Stanford University.

Murray, S. C. (2017). *The Collapse of the Mycenaean Economy: Imports, Trade, and Institutions 1300–700 BCE*. Cambridge: Cambridge University Press.

Murray, S. C. (2023). *Long-Distance Exchange and Inter-Regional Economies*. Cambridge Elements. The Aegean Bronze Age. Cambridge: Cambridge University Press.

Murray, S. C., & Lis, B. (2023). Documenting a maritime mercantile community through surface survey: Porto Rafti Bay in the post-collapse Aegean. *Antiquity* **97(393)**, 1–7, Article e13.

Nakassis, D. (2006). *The Individual and the Mycenaean State: Agency and Prosopography in the Linear B Texts from Pylos* (Ph.D. dissertation, The University of Texas at Austin).

Nakassis, D. (2013). *Individuals and Society in Mycenaean Pylos* (Mnemosyne Supplements, History and Archaeology of Classical Antiquity 358). Boston: Brill.

Nakassis, D. (2015). Labor and individuals in Late Bronze Age Pylos. In P. Steinkeller, & M. Hudson, eds., *Labor in the Ancient World: Volume V.* Dresden: ISLET-Verlag, pp. 583–616.

Nitsch, E. K., Jones, G., Sarpaki, A., Hald, M. M., & Bogaard, A. (2019). Farming practice and land management at Knossos, Crete: New insights from $\delta13C$ and $\delta15N$ Analysis of Neolithic and Bronze Age crop remains. In D. Garcia, R. Orgeolet, M. Pomadère, & J. Zurbach, eds., *Country in the City: Agricultural Functions in Protohistoric Urban Settlements (Aegean and Western Mediterranean)*. Oxford: Archaeopress, pp. 152–68.

Nobis, G. (1991). Das Gastmahl des Nestor, Herrscher über Pylos. Mythos und Wahrheit über mykenische Tafelfreuden. *Tier und Museum* **2(3)**, pp. 67–77.

Nosch, M.-L. (2000a). *The Organization of the Mycenaean Textile Industry* (Ph. D. dissertation Salzburg 2000).

Nosch, M.-L. (2000b). Acquisition and distribution: *ta-ra-si-ja* in the Mycenaean textile industry. In C. Gillis, C. Risberg, & B. Sjöberg, eds., *Trade and Production in Premonetary Greece: Acquisition and Distribution of Raw Materials and Finished Products: Proceedings of the 6th International*

Workshop, Athens 1996, Jonsered, Paul Åströms Förlag, SIMA-PB 154, pp. 43–61.

Nosch, M.-L. (2006). More thoughts on the Mycenaean *ta-ra-si-ja* system. In M. Perna, ed., *Fiscality in Mycenaean and Near Eastern Archives: Proceedings of the Conference Held at Soprintendenza Archivistica per la Campania, Nampes, 21–23 October 2004*. Paris: de Boccard, 161–82.

Nosch, M.-L. (2012). From texts to textiles in the Aegean Bronze Age. In M.-L. Nosch, & R. Laffineur, eds., *KOSMOS: Jewellery, Adornment and Textiles in the Aegean Bronze Age: Proceedings of the 13th International Aegean Conference* (Aegaeum 33). Louven: Peeters, pp. 43–55.

Nosch, M.-L. (2014). Mycenaean wool economies in the latter part of the second millennium BC Aegean. In C. Breniquet & C. Michel, eds., *Wool Economy in the Ancient Near East and the Aegean*. Oxford: Oxbow, pp. 371–400.

Nosch, M.-L. B., & Perna, M. (2001). Cloth in the cult. In R. Laffineur, & R. Hägg, eds., *Potnia: Deities and Religion in the Aegean Bronze Age: 8th International Aegean Conference, University of Göteborg, 12–15 April 2000* (Aegaeum 22). Austin: The University of Texas at Austin, pp. 471–77.

Ntinou, M., Karanthou, A., Pagnoux, C., & Valamoti, S.-M. (2022). Land management and food resources in Bronze Age central Greece: Insights from archaeobotanical assemblages from the sites of Agia Paraskevi, Kynos, and Mitrou (Phthiotida). In Valamoti, S.-M., A. Dimoula, & M. Ntinou, eds., *Cooking with Plants*. Leiden: Sidestone Press, pp. 71–91.

Olivier, J.-P. (1987). Structure des archives palatiales en linéaire A et en linéaire B. In *Le Système Palatial en Orient, en Grèce et à Rome: Actes du Colloque de Strasbourg (19–22 Juin 1985)*. Leyden: E. J. Brill, pp. 227–35.

Olivier, J.-P. (1988). KN:Da-Dg. In J.-P. Olivier, & T. G. Palaima, eds., *Texts, Tablets and Scribes: Studies in Mycenaean Epigraphy and Economy: Offered to Emmett L. Bennett, Jr., MINOS* (Supplement 10). Pisa: Ediciones Universidad de Salamanca Servicio editorial, pp. 219–67.

Olivier, J.-P. (2024). Syllabic scripts in the Aegean and Cyprus in the second and first millennia. In J. Killen, ed., *The New Documents in Mycenaean Greek*. Cambridge: Cambridge University Press, pp. 49–94.

Oliver, J.-P., & Godart, L. (1996). *Corpus Hieroglyphicarum Inscriptionum Cretae*. Paris: De Boccard, École Française d'Athènes (Etudes Crétoises, 31).

Palaima, T. G. (1989). Perspectives on the Pylos oxen tablets: Textual (and archaeological) evidence for the use and management of oxen in Late Bronze Age Messenia (and Crete). In T. G. Palaima, C. W. Shelmerdine, & P. Hr. Ilievski, eds., *Studia Mycenaea 1988* (Ziva Antika Monograph 7). Skopje: University of Skopje, pp. 85–124.

Palaima, T. G. (1991). Maritime matters in the Linear B tablets. In R. Laffineur, & L. Basch, eds., *Thalassa: L'Egée préhistorique et la mer: Actes de la troisième rencontre égéenne internationale de l' Université de Liège, Station de recherches sous-marines et océanographiques (StaReSo), Calvi, Corse, 23–25 avril 1990* (Aegaeum 7). Austin: The University of Texas at Austin, pp. 273–310.

Palaima, T. G. (1992). The Knossos oxen dossier. In J.-P. Olivier, ed., *Mykenaïka: Actes du IXe Colloque international sur les textes mycéniens et égéens organisé par le Centre de l'Antiquité Grecque et Romaine de la Fondation Hellénique des Recherches Scientifiques et l'École Française d'Athènes, Athènes, 2–6 octobre 1990* (BCH Supplement 25). Paris: De Boccard, pp. 463–74.

Palaima, T. G. (1994). Seal-users and script-users/nodules and tablets at LMIB Hagia Triada. In P. Ferioli, E. Fiandra, G.G. Fissore, and M. Frangipane eds., *Archives before Writing: Proceedings of the International Colloquium, Oriolo Romano, October 23–25, 1991*. Rome: Ministero per i beni culturali e ambientali, Ufficio centrale per i beni archivistici, pp. 307–30.

Palaima, T. G. (1997). Potter and fuller: The royal craftsmen. In R. Laffineur, & P. Betancourt, eds., *TEXNH: Craftsmen, Craftswomen and Craftsmanship in the Aegean Bronze Age: Proceedings of the 6th International Aegean Conference, Philadelphia, Temple University, 18–21 April 1996* (Aegaeum 16). Austin: Université de Liège and University of Texas at Austin, pp. 407–12.

Palaima, T. (2014). Pylos tablet Vn 130 and the Pylos perfume industry. In D. Nakassis, J. Gulizio, & S. James, eds., *KE-RA-ME-JA: Studies Presented to Cynthia Shelmerdine*. Philadelphia, PA: INSTAP, pp. 83–90.

Palmer, R. (1989). Subsistence rations at Pylos and Knossos. *Minos* **24**, 89–124.

Palmer, R. (1992). Wheat and barley in Mycenaean society. In J.-P. Olivier, ed., *Mykenaïka: Actes du IX' Colloque international sur les textes mycéniens et égéens, Athènes, 2–6 octobre 1990 (BCH Suppl. XXV 1992)*. Paris: De Boccard, pp. 475–97.

Palmer, R. (1994). *Wine in the Mycenaean Palace Economy*. Aegaeum 10. Liège: Université de Liège.

Palmer, R. (1995). Linear A commodities: A comparison of resources. In R. Laffineur, & W.-D. Niemeier, eds., *POLITEIA: Society and State in the Aegean Bronze Age: Proceedings of the 5th International Aegean Conference, Heidelberg, 10–13 April 1994 (Aegaeum 12)*. Austin: University of Texas at Austin, pp. 133–56.

Palmer, R. (1999). Perishable goods in Mycenaean texts. In S. Deger-Jalkotzy, S. Hiller, & O. Panagl, eds., *Floreant Studia Mycenaea: Akten des X. Internationalen Mykenologischen Colloquiums in Salzberg Vom 1.-5.*

Mai 1995. Band II. Wein: Verlag der Osterreichischen Akademie der Wissenschaften, pp. 463–85.

Palmer, R. (2001). Bridging the gap: The continuity of Greek agriculture from the Mycenaean to the historical period. In D. W. Tandy, ed., *Prehistory and History: Ethnicity, Class and Political Economy.* Montreal: Black Rose Books, pp. 41–84.

Palmer, R. (2002). Wine in Minoan Crete: The textual evidence. In Aik. Mylopotamitaki, ed., *Oinos Palaios Idypotos: To Kritiko Krasi apo ta Proïstorika os ta Neotera Chronia. Kounavoi: Dimos 'N. Kazantzakis', 24– 26 Apriliou 1998.* Irakleio: Ypourgeio Politismou Archaiologiko Institouto Kritis, Praktika tou Diethnous Epistimonikou Symposiou, pp. 95–103.

Palmer, R. (2008). Wheat and barley in Mycenaean society 15 years later. In A. Sacconi, M. Del Freo, L. Godart, & M. Negri, eds., *Colloquium Romanum: atti del XII Colloquia internazionale di micenologia: Roma, 20–25 febbraio 2006.* Pisa: F. Serra, pp. 621–39.

Pasternak, R. (2006). Bericht zu den archäobotanische Funde aus Stadt-Nordost. *Archäologischer Anzeiger* **2006**, 134–38.

Perna, M. (2005). L'alun dans les documents en linéaire B. In P. Borgard, J.-P. Brun, & M. Picon, eds., *L'alun de Méditerranée, colloque international, Naples 4–6 juin, Lipari 7–8 juin 2003.* Naples: De Boccard, pp. 39–42.

Perna, M. (2014). The birth of administration and writing in Minoan Crete: Some thoughts on hieroglyphics and Linear A. In D. Nakassis, J. Gulizio, & S. A. James, eds., *KE-RA-ME-JA: Studies Presented to Cynthia W. Shelmerdine.* Philadelphia, PA: INSTAP Academic Press, pp. 251–59.

Piteros,C., J.-P. Olivier, & J. L. Melena. (1990). "Les inscriptions en Linéaire B des nodules de Thèbes (1982): La fouille, les documents, les possibilites d'interpretation." *BCH* **104**, 103–84.

Platon, L., & Kopaka, K. (1993). Linoi Minoikoi: Installations minoennes de traitement des produits liquides. *Bulletin de Correspondance Hellenique* **177** (**1**), 35–101.

Platon, N. (1971). *Zakros: The Discovery of a Lost Palace of Ancient Crete.* New York: Scribner.

Popham, M. R., & Sackett, L. H. (1968). *Excavations at Lefkandi, Euboea 1964–1966.* London: Thames & Hudson.

Pratt, C. E. (2016). The rise and fall of the transport stirrup jar in the Bronze Age Aegean. *American Journal of Archaeology* **120**(**1**), 27–66.

Pratt, C. E. (2021). *Oil, Wine and the Cultural Economy of Ancient Greece: From the Bronze Age to the Archaic Era.* New York: Cambridge University Press.

Rougemont, F. (2004). Flax and linen textiles in the Mycenaean palatial economy. In M. Perna, ed., *Recherches sur la fiscalité mycénienne*. Paris: De Boccard, pp. 46–49.

Rougemont, F. (2009). *Contrôle économique et administration à l'époque des palais mycéniens (fin du IIe millénaire av. J.-C.)*. Athens: Ecole française d'Athènes.

Salgarella, E. (2020). *Aegean Linear Script(s): Rethinking the Relationship between Linear A and Linear B*. Cambridge: Cambridge University Press.

Sarpaki, A. (2007). Résultats archéobotaniques préliminaires dans divers secteurs de Malia. *Bulletin de Correspondance Hellénique* **131(2)**, 882–84.

Sarpaki, A., & Bending, J. (2004). Archaeobotanical assemblages. In J. S. Soles, T. Brogan, C. Frederick, et al., eds., *Mochlos IC. Period III. Neopalatial Settlement on the Coast: The Artisans' Quarter and the Farmhouse at Chalinomouri. The Small Finds* (Prehistory Monographs 9). Philadelphia, PA: INSTAP Academic Press, pp 126–31.

Schachl, R. (2006). Die archäobotanischen Reste. In E. Alram-Stern, & S. Deger-Jalkotzy, eds., *Aigeira I, Die Mykenische Akropolis, Faszikel 3*. Vienna: Verlag der Österreichischen Akademie der Wissenschaften, pp. 189–201.

Schoep, I. (2002). *The Administration of Neopalatial Crete: A Critical Assessment of the Linear A Tablets and Their Role in the Administrative Process*. MINOS suppl. 17. Salamanca: Ediciones Universidad de Salamanca.

Shelmerdine, C. W. (1973). The Pylos Ma tablets reconsidered. *American Journal of Archaeology* **77**, 261–75.

Shelmerdine, C. W. (1985). *The Perfume Industry in Mycenaean Pylos*. SIMA-PB 34. Göteborg: Paul Åströms Förlag.

Shelmerdine, C. W. (1988). Mycenaean taxation. In T. G. Palaima, C. W. Shelmerdine, & P. H. Ilievski, eds., *Studia Mycenaea 1988* (ZivaAnt Monograph 7). Austin: The University of Texas at Austin, pp. 125–48.

Sherratt, A. (1993). Who are you calling peripheral? Dependence and independence in European prehistory. In C. Scarre & F. Healy, eds., *Trade and Exchange in Prehistoric Europe*. Oxford: Oxbow, pp. 245–55.

Sherratt, S. (1981). *The Pottery of LHIIIC and Its Significance*. Ph.D. dissertation, University of Oxford.

Smith, J. S. (1992–93 [1995]). The Pylos Jn series. *Minos* **27–28**, 167–259.

Soles, J. S. (2003). *Mochlos IA. Period III. Neopalatial Settlement on the Coast: The Artisan's Quarter and the Farmhouse at Chalinomouri. The Site* (Prehistory Monographs 7), Philadelphia, PA: INSTAP Academic Press.

Soles, J. S. (2004). New construction at Mochlos in the LM IB period. In L. P. Day, M. S. Mook, & J. D. Muhly, eds., *Crete beyond the Palaces: Proceedings of the Crete 2000 Conference* (Prehistory Monographs 10). Philadelphia, PA: INSTAP Academic Press, pp. 153–62.

Stanley, P. V. (1999). Gradation and quality of wines in the Greek and Roman worlds. *Journal of Wine Research* **19(2)**, 105–14.

Steele, P. M. (2024). *Exploring Writing Systems and Practices in the Bronze Age Aegean*. Oxford: Oxbow Books.

Stocker, S., & Davis, J. (2004). Animal sacrifice, archives, and feasting at the Palace of Nestor. *The Mycenaean Feast: Hesperia* **73(2)**, 179–95.

Thomatos, M. (2006). *The Final Revival of the Aegean Bronze Age: A Case Study of the Argolid, Corinthia, Attica, Euboea, the Cyclades and the Dodecanese during LH IIIC Middle*. BAR-IS 1498. Oxford: Archaeopress.

Thompson, R. J. E. (2010). In defense of ideograms. In P. Carlier, C. de Lamberterie, M. Egetmeyer, et al., eds., *Études mycéniennes 2010: actes du XIIIe Colloque international sur les textes égéens: Sèvres, Paris, Nanterre, 20–23 septembre 2010*. Pisa: F. Serra, pp. 545–61.

Tsafou, E., & García-Granero, J. J. (2021). Beyond staple crops: Exploring the use of "invisible" plant ingredients in Minoan cuisine through starch grain analysis on ceramic vessels. *Archaeological and Anthropological Sciences* **13**, 128.

Tzachili, I. (2001). Circulation of textiles in the Late Bronze Age Aegean. In A. Michailidou, ed., *Manufacture and Measurement, Counting, Measuring and Recording Craft Items in Early Aegean Societies*. Athens: Research Centre for Greek and Roman Antiquity, National Hellenic Research Foundation, pp. 167–75.

Valamoti, S. M., Dimoula, A., Ntinou, M., eds. (2022). *Cooking with Plants in Ancient Europe and Beyond*. Leiden: Sidestone Press.

van Wijngaarden, G. J. (2002). *Use and Appreciation of Mycenaean Pottery in the Levant, Cyprus, and Italy (1600–1200 BC)*. Amsterdam: Amsterdam University Press.

Varias García, C. (2012). The word for "honey" and connected terms in Mycenaean Greek. In P. Carlier, C. de Lamberterie, M. Egetmeyer, et al., eds., *Études mycéniennes 2010 : actes du XIIIe Colloque international sur les textes égéens : Sèvres, Paris, Nanterre, 20–23 septembre 2010*. Pisa: F. Serra, pp. 403–18.

Ventris, M. (2024). Discovery and decipherment. In J. Killen, ed., *The New Documents in Mycenaean Greek*. Cambridge: Cambridge University Press, pp. 25–48.

Ventris, M., & Chadwick, J. (1973). *Documents in Mycenaean Greek* (2nd ed). Cambridge: Cambridge University Press.

Vokotopoulos, L., Plath, G., & McCoy, F. W. (2014). The yield of the land: Soil conservation and the exploitation of arable land at Choiromandres, Zakros in the New Palace period. In G. Touchais, R. Laffineur, & F. Rougemont, eds., *Physis* (Aegaeum 37). Liège: Louven, pp. 251–63.

Wace, A. J. B. (1921– 1923). Excavations at Mycenae VII: The lion gate and grave circle area. *Annual of the British School at Athens* **25**, 9–126.

Wallace, S. (2000). Case studies of settlement change in Early Iron Age Crete. *AeA* **4**, 61–99.

Watrous, L. V., & Heimroth, A. (2011). Household industries of Late Minoan IB: Gournia and the socioeconomic status of the town. In K. T. Glowacki, & N. Vogeikoff-Brogan, eds., *Stega: The Archaeoloogy of Houses and Households in Ancient Crete*. Hesperia Supplement 44. Princeton, NJ: The American School of Classical Studies at Athens, pp. 199–212.

Weilhartner, J. (2005). *Mykenische Opfergaben: nach Aussage der Linear B – Texte*. Wien: Verlag der Österreichischen Akademie der Wissenschaften.

Whitelaw, T. (2001). Reading between the tablets: Assessing Mycenaean palatial involvement in ceramic production and consumption. In S. Voutsaki, & J. Killen, eds., *Economy and Politics in the Mycenaean Palace States*. Cambridge: Cambridge Philological Society, pp. 51–79.

Wood, J., Hsu, Y.-T., & Bell, C. (2021). Sending Laurion back to the future: Bronze Age silver and the source of confusion. *Internet Archaeology* **56**, 9.

Cambridge Elements ≡

The Aegean Bronze Age

Carl Knappett

University of Toronto

Carl Knappett is the Walter Graham/ Homer Thompson Chair in Aegean Prehistory at the University of Toronto.

Irene Nikolakopoulou

Hellenic Ministry of Culture, Archaeological Museum of Heraklion

Irene Nikolakopoulou is an archaeologist and curator at the Archaeological Museum of Heraklion, Crete.

About the Series

This series is devised thematically to foreground the conceptual developments in the Aegean Bronze Age, one of the richest subfields of archaeology, while reflecting the range of institutional settings in which research in this field is conducted. It aims to produce an innovative and comprehensive review of the latest scholarship in Aegean prehistory.

Cambridge Elements ☰

The Aegean Bronze Age

Elements in the Series

Long-Distance Exchange and Inter-Regional Economies
Sarah C. Murray

Aegeomania: Modern Reimaginings of the Aegean Bronze Age
Nicoletta Momigliano

Economy and Commodity Production in the Aegean Bronze Age
Catherine E. Pratt

A full series listing is available at: www.cambridge.org/EABA